FINDING

SUCCESS

IN SPITE OF THE MESS

LAMAN CG SNYDER

ARPress

ARPress
45 Dan Road Suite 5
Canton MA 02021

| Hotline: | 1(888) 821-0229 |
| Fax: | 1(508) 545-7580 |

Ordering Information:

Quantity sales. Special discounts are available on quantity purchases by corporations, associations, and others. For details, contact the publisher at the address above.

Printed in the United States of America.

| ISBN-13: | Softcover | 979-8-89389-081-5 |
| | eBook | 979-8-89389-082-2 |

Library of Congress Control Number: 2024911430

TABLE OF CONTENTS

Dedication

Developing this book was a labor of love and pride, which is what every job should be. That has been my pathway through everything I set out to accomplish in life – enjoy it, have fun, and be proud of the mission. I have had a wonderful career in Human Resources leadership. My purpose going to work every day was to help others achieve their business and career objectives. I truly believe that is why I was put on this earth – to help make other people better. I am writing this book to share some of my experience and philosophy, hopefully inspire others to find success and fulfillment, and offer some practical steps to make achieving your dreams a possibility.

You can't do many worthy tasks alone; indeed, why would you want to. There are many people who have inspired me through my life, and I am grateful to each one them. There are a few who deserve a special thanks. Robert Weaver of HR For HIRE, for successfully continuing and expanding the mission of the business I founded. Jim Swanson, CEO of Kitchell Corporation. I have worked with many great leaders, Jim is one of the finest. Jim puts true meaning to an open door policy, and every employee can not only talk to him, they can disagree with him. Jim and I spend a lot of time questioning and challenging each other, and always seem to come up with a better answer. Patrick Bosworth of Leadership Choice; the source of our communication training and also a person who goes the extra mile for the Human Resources community. Jack Milligan of Leathers, Milligan & Associates; someone I have relied on for a variety of consulting services, and we also share our passion for helping others in Human Resources. Jack deservedly won the SHRM of Arizona, Al O'Connor Lifetime Achievement Award. I was a finalist. I considered it a huge honor to be considered in the same category with Jack. Patrick, Jack and I were all good friends of the late Al O'Connor, and I certainly want to include Al in my dedications. Al was an inspiration to us and so many others. And a special thanks to Jeff Thoren and Sally Stamp of Gifted Leaders; who helped us design and facilitate our Leadership Development curriculum which has brought us so much success and acclaim. All of the above mentioned people have affected positive change in many people's lives. They certainly made an impact on mine.

But my true guiding light is my wonderful wife Denise, who is always by my side to give me encouragement and share her keen sense for seeing the other perspective. We are a great balancing act.

I also want to dedicate this book to our daughter Stacie, our son Cory, and our three precious grandchildren Taylor, Cole and Emma.

Foreword

"Never doubt that a small group of people with a commitment to a common purpose can change the world. Indeed, it is the only thing that ever has." -Margaret Mead

My purpose for this book is to share things I've learned through a wealth of career experiences. I will present a set of ingredients for personal fulfillment, and a set of guidelines for team excellence, which should be applicable to business teams, sports teams, volunteer groups, and so on. So if you are a business leader, an aspiring contributor with career goals, or involved with your child's baseball team or scout troop; you will hopefully find this book to be helpful.

I am closing my career with a great employee-owned company, Kitchell Corporation, headquartered in Phoenix, Arizona. Known mostly for commercial construction, we are diversified in various lines of business. The company has a strong culture, many talented people, and the best HR team I have had the privilege of working with throughout my career. Kitchell has a purpose statement which can be seen everywhere – on company trucks, hard hats, signage, intranet…everywhere. It simply states, "Together, Building Value Every Day." A small but powerful reminder that we exist to build, or contribute, something – create something of lasting value for our customers; and the key word is "Together." We are doing it with pride and professionalism, as a team. Before I joined Kitchell I often heard the phrase, "an employee-owned company." I wasn't really sure what that meant, other than participation in a profit sharing or private stock program. However, it really does create an atmosphere of inclusion. Everyone is a stakeholder and feels ownership in all aspects of the company. Everyone can make a difference. We have a section on the company intranet titled What You Do Matters, where people share stories of employee achievements that made a positive impact.

People are the building blocks, the foundation, and the most important assets. We've all heard it, seen it, read it. Why is it true at some places, where the culture is built around it, and decisions are based on it; while at other places the words are shallow, insulting, and a waste of the paper they are written on? We are all products of our experiences and of those we emulate. We can learn as much from a bad boss as we can from a good boss. I've had some of each. I have had experiences with some people, either a direct manager or a powerful position holder in the organization, who could play a villain in most any movie. Not a role model for sure, but we can learn lessons from them – we remember what we won't be like when we are in that position.

A good person of influence, whether they be a manager, teacher, coach, parent, big brother, or anyone we have associated with, is of course an ideal person to emulate, and we have done that automatically through our whole lives. We should always be aware of our environment, and good or bad, make it a learning experience.

We are all familiar with the old expression, "All is fair in love and war." Meaning there are no rules in competition for romance, or in the engagement of warfare. Although the old expression has stuck, we all know that the statement is untrue. Indeed, there are many laws, ethics and customs which define unacceptable actions in both love and war. Then we look at the workplace. We can find things unfair in our work environment on any given day. Someone is getting special treatment with their training or assignment; another is getting away with frequently leaving early when that same standard doesn't apply to coworkers. We could give countless examples. I have seen and dealt with many. Sometimes we corrected the situation. Sometimes the situation was not wrong, even quite rational and logical, just perceived as unfair. Those situations were often explained, understood, and accepted. Communication is a wonderful thing. Sometimes the action was just a hard business decision that had to be made, which the disgruntled party will never find reasonable, but was within the scope of management to do it. Now you must get past it and move on. The title of this book is Finding Success In Spite Of The Mess. I will share techniques on how to do just that – move on and be successful.

The sequence of this book follows the development plan we instituted at Kitchell – first, leading yourself; then leading your team. We all have occasion to participate on teams, and sometimes have the designation of team leader. Whether it be the whole company, a department, a project, a social or charity function, a community or school organization – most work gets done through the united efforts of team members. Therefore, we must be adept at team skills, whatever our role happens to be. However, in order to become a dynamic team leader, or valued contributor, we must first find personal success and fulfillment. Self-awareness and self-motivation are prerequisites to leading others. You cannot be an inspiration to other people if you do not have happiness and confidence in yourself.

I am convinced that most people are dedicated to their career, and want to be successful for themselves and earn the appreciation of others. People do not get up in the morning and think, "I'm going to go in there today and do a lousy job and aggravate my boss." Rather, they want to make a positive contribution, do their job well, earn the respect of management and coworkers, and help the company succeed. Likewise, most managers do not start their day with the thought of "I'm going to find mistakes and get on someone's case today!" They too want the day to run smoothly, want people to be happy and motivated, and want success and recognition for their team. The intent of this book is to help that all unfold, by removing the barriers and avoiding the misunderstandings.

Most people come to work focused on self and task. They don't ask themselves, "What's my boss, or anyone else for that matter, going to do for me today?" Rather, they know they are there to do their job, and hope they eventually get recognized. Most managers don't set their top priority to see if they can generate recognition, bonuses and promotions for their people – their top priority has to be the success of their function and its contribution to the company. Then the recognition and rewards will follow. The role of Human Resources is to be a catalyst to make job enrichment happen. We want people to come to work eager and happy to be there, enjoy their job and work environment, and go home satisfied – not frustrated. Sure, we all have a bad day once in a while, but it is unacceptable if that is the norm. We are optimistic enough to believe this is attainable at all levels, and will positively affect company success and profitability.

Life, in and out of work, should be exciting, fun and challenging. We cannot prevent every action we may perceive as unfair; but we can learn how to be more accepting and tolerant, and we can especially find ways to keep ourselves above the fray and overcome all barriers to our success.

Chapter 1

Kid's Games

"Every man is part boy, and every boy is part man."
- Chief Brave Eagle

FIND THE THINGS THAT DON'T BELONG

One of the fun games I used to love doing as a child, and later with little kids, was the exercise in a children's activity book called Find the Things That Don't Belong. We would find a clock on the wall with the numbers backwards, a person wearing a shirt with sleeves of different lengths, a table with a leg missing, and of course the inevitable fish out of water. I never thought of it as a game that prepared me for life, but I have spent a long career in Human Resources doing just that – finding the things that don't fit.

Sometimes it's a person who just does not fit in – with their coworkers, their supervisor, the team, the company, the industry....or customers! Then we gather all the smarter people to make a decision – is this person salvageable, can we reinvent them, improve their skills, explain to them that they must change their personality, make them (insert company name here) material. And of course, to ensure there are no misunderstandings, because we will give them all the support we possibly can, let's document this in writing and give them 90 days to turn things around. Sound familiar, how's your success rate?

Have you ever been that person? You know, the one who felt like a fish out of water. Maybe you weren't ready for this job. Maybe you were more than qualified for the job description, but were not informed of the demands on your lifestyle. Maybe you were just not expecting that your new boss would emulate the style of a Marine Drill Sergeant.

How do people get into these situations? How do we prevent them from happening in the future? Can they ever be fixed? Well, fortunately there is hope. Situations like this occur every day, and you have likely been involved in more than one. While business calamities often go beyond the people, some person or team usually shoulders the blame.

The business itself may not belong. Businesses tend to evolve. They must. And in doing so they often lose sight of their roots – their purpose, their values, their loyal customers and their dedicated employees. I have seen many small businesses start, grind, adjust, find success and prosper. Next, out of necessity they experience growth. Growth too fast to prepare; above the level of their business acumen; taking opportunities outside of their expertise; and they soon become the fish out of water. They don't know what they don't know. So they just don't concern themselves with trivial things like workplace legislation, copyright infringements, customer appreciation. The business becomes about the royal family, not about employees, customers, vendors or suppliers.

These ills are certainly not limited to small businesses. In larger venues they are simply done on a larger scale and spread throughout the organization. There are more places to hide, and more places to be pointing fingers.

Now don't start thinking all companies are guilty of being work dungeons. There are just as many great places to work as there are poor ones, and I actually think the trend is positive. Workplace laws and customer demands require it, and people at all levels are better informed as to the expectations of their customers, their workforce, their stakeholders, and the general public. Communication has become more transparent, informative, available, and fast.

We can live and be successful in this new business climate. We can find enjoyment and enrichment. All we have to do is find the things that don't belong – and fix them.

FOLLOW THE LEADER

Another popular kid's game I remember was an outdoor activity called Follow the Leader. We follow and do as the Leader does, as he or she performs increasingly foolish or daring things. When you finally refuse to go any further and stop performing, the Leader wins. I think we can see the business correlation here already. How many times have you seen others follow a Leader when everyone knew the Leader was wrong? Did you follow? Who was brave enough to stand up to the Leader and tell him or her that they are wrong and we will not follow. Are they still with the firm? It takes a brave and confident person to say "Stop! This is not right. We need a new course of action."

But the game rules were clear. The Leader is in charge. The Leader does what he or she feels, and sets the degree of difficulty. Some Leaders were very daring and did things that nobody could keep up with. After a while, that was no fun. It made everyone not want to play anymore when Butch was the leader. Then there were Leaders who were always too timid, which was no fun either. That got boring. The best Leaders made it fun and kept everyone engaged. We all had laughs and wanted to play some more. And next time when someone suggested playing Follow the Leader, we all yelled for Van or Rodney or Judy to be the Leader.

Leaders can intimidate and scare their followers, or they can engage them and gain their trust and allegiance. It is as true and predictable in business culture today as it was in kid's games years before. So simple that it raises the question, why would any kid, or manager, want to be a bully who gets people to follow them through fear and intimidation, when the alternative is more productive, more enjoyable, and earns admiration?

PIN THE TAIL ON THE DONKEY

A standard at all birthday parties when I was a child. A picture of a donkey without a tail was hung on the wall. Each child was given a paper tail with a thumbtack in it. Then you were blindfolded, turned around, and pointed in the direction of the donkey. Your direction was somewhat guided by the yells and laughter of the other kids watching. After you mounted your tail, you removed the blindfold, and saw the results of your placement. In the end, tails were all over the place, and the person whose tail was placed closest to the proper position was the winner.

The analogy to the business world is maybe too easy, maybe too frightening. A: The picture on the wall just might be the one of your current manager, who may be a real jackass. B: People might be expected to show blind loyalty to the leader and do whatever they can to make him or her look better. And C: Just as the kids were pinning tails on both the head and the rear end, some may wonder from which end the leader is doing their thinking.

HIDE AND SEEK

This was a fun and active game. More fun outdoors than inside, and more fun in the evening when it was starting to get dark. Yes, we could play outside with flashlights in those days. Everyone would hide, and the person whose turn it was would try to find them. When discovered, both would run back to the base, and the first person to touch the base would win. If the one hiding got there first, he was home safe. If the seeker reached the base first, he got you. This repeated until everyone was accounted for. Then someone else got their turn, and everyone else would hide.

You didn't have to wait to be found. When the seeker moved away from the base, you could make a run for it, and if you touched the base before being discovered, you were home safe.

So you either stayed in hiding until you were discovered, then had to race to the base; or you could hide and sneak up to the base without being discovered.

Some employees spend a lot of their work time hiding – low key, below the radar, hoping they don't get questioned. I'm not saying they don't do any work, but they are afraid of taking any risks, of having to justify what they are doing. Better to play it safe and stay in hiding until the boss wanders off, then submit your work without any discussion. These are people who are not in the game for the excitement or fulfillment; rather, they are just putting in their time, doing their assigned job duties, and can't wait for the day to end.

SIMON SAYS

A favorite game that has been around for centuries where everyone faces the leader, who issues commands. If you don't follow the leader's commands exactly, you are out. If you start before the leader states "Simon Says" you are out. The leader's objective is to observe anyone not following his or her exact command or starting without the official word, and eliminate them. Thus, you are told what to do and when to do it or you are discharged. Ever work in a place like that?

MUSICAL CHAIRS

We all walk around in circles until the music stops, then we quickly sit in a chair. Someone is eliminated each round because there is always one chair short. Warped value learned here – get aggressive and grab, don't share. If you ever had a job where they took away your office or work station, think of it as musical chairs.

PLAYING DOCTOR

Playing doctor, or fireman, or teacher, or cowboy, or soldier, or astronaut, or cop. We all did our thing as kids, and probably went from one to another, as we moved through different phases. And our parents gave full support to our fantasies by getting us the necessary costumes, toys and props. And it wasn't just what we wanted to play, it was what we wanted to be. Children want to be a basketball player, or a race car driver, or Bob the Builder, or Dora the Explorer. And with small children, parents are very accommodating.

Then children start to get a little older, and somewhere in the grade school or middle school range, negative influences start to interfere with their childhood fantasies. From who? Their parents. They are told they cannot become a famous singer or actress or athlete or astronaut. And told they really do not want to be a fireman or chef or plumber. It's time they start to grow up and think more mature and live into the role their parents have set for them, or at least one which their parents will approve. Parents start beating down their dreams and start to mold them into what parents determine is their destiny.

This pounding down of dreams can get pretty ingrained. As these children grow up they are accustomed to what they cannot accomplish. "I can't go back to school and get a degree, I can't start my own business, and I can't get promoted."

Somehow, we have become our own barrier to our dreams and goals. We have to regain the carefree innocence of youth and once again make work and play come together.

Do we really need to give up on our dreams and desires? Hopefully not. While going to work every day may not be a game, it certainly should not be a war. Everyone has a bad day once in a while. But no one should go to work every day unhappy with their job, and come home frustrated every night. If you dislike what you do – then do something else. If you have lost faith in your company's values, find a place of employment that has values better aligned with your own. If you are unappreciated, do an honest evaluation of your worthiness, and either improve your contribution, make yourself known, or move on. If you are being mistreated or bullied by someone, do something about them.

You made it through childhood, through school, now let's make it through career and life.

Chapter 2

The Old West

"All the screen cowboys behaved like real gentlemen. They didn't drink, they didn't smoke. When they knocked a bad guy down, they always stood with their fists up, waiting for the heavy to get back on his feet." - John Wayne

There is so much to be learned from old westerns. If you are lucky enough to remember the era when westerns dominated movies, television shows and comic books, they probably have made an influence on your life. Unlike today's movies, television shows and video games with all their violence, blood, torture, explosions and other special effects; with stories about drug gangs, crooked police, supernatural heroes, and space aliens. The old westerns were simple. It was good guys against bad guys. And you knew right away who they were. The good guys wore white hats, often rode a white horse, and always achieved justice and got the girl at the end. The bad guys wore black hats, were generally not very smart, and fought dirty – usually picked up a knife, threw a chair (always missed), and had a partner hold the good guy's arms from behind. Didn't matter, our hero always won at the end.

The stories made a clear influence on youth of right vs. wrong. Good guys had values; bad guys were crooks. Good guys helped the poor innocent victims, whom the bad guys had cheated and robbed.

Peaceful town folk usually included the proprietor of the general store, the doctor, the saloon keeper, the preacher, the newspaper editor, and other various merchants, ranchers and farmers. The sinister evil villains were often the banker, the land baron, the railroad, and the rustlers. Sheriffs were 50-50. There were good sheriffs and bad sheriffs, depending on the story. But if they called him a marshal, then he was on the good side.

Notice who was usually on the good column – small business. And who was on the notorious bad side – big business. Even in the old westerns, big business was identified with money, power, and corruption.

As for work ethic, they didn't show us much. In some shows the heroes actually had jobs as lawmen (marshals), such as Gunsmoke and Wyatt Earp. Some were ranch owners, like Bonanza and High Chaparral. But most didn't work – they just roamed into town, saw wrong doing, fixed it, and then rode away at the end. They went from town to town to make the old west a better place. If bad guys went from town to town they were referred to as drifters. Good guys roamed into town. So good guys were roamers; bad guys were drifters. We learned perception can be all in the title.

We also learned about prejudice. Tonto and Chief Brave Eagle showed us that Indians could be wise, trusted and on the side of justice. The Cisco Kid did the same for Mexicans. These were early examples of breaking old stereotypes, which were a good influence on youth. And for really changing prejudice, how about The Lone Ranger and Zorro being heroes to the impoverished, yet wearing black masks to hide their identity. The older people of the town always assumed the masked man was there to rob them, but we kids knew better – we knew there was a good person behind the mask. The show always ended with a morale message about judging a person on his honesty and values, not on his appearance. Yes, the cowboys taught us great life lessons.

I refer to the Old West, rather than the Wild West. The Old West was actually a wonderful time and place. People were adventurous and settling in a new land of opportunity, government was trying to expand the country and establish law and order, business and commerce were encouraging and funding the growth, and everyone was utilizing our abundance of natural resources and living off the land. City life was developing and in many areas flourishing; building stores, hotels, churches, and other enterprise. Even communications were advancing with newspapers, mail service and telegraph.

Folklore depicts the era as the Wild West, when there was danger all around, lawlessness and corruption were commonplace, most people carried firearms, and there were shootings in the streets. But that was not the true old west, that sounds more like our nation today.

Why did the old westerns fade away? For years Hollywood has been trying to bring back the westerns, with little success. Probably because they make them to today's production standards with violence, gore and special effects. Scenes with the barroom brawls of no one getting hurt, people taking bullets with no blood spilled, shooting the gun out of the bad guy's hand with no injury, bad guys shot dead but not shown after falling off of the horse, would probably be boring today, even for the children's audience.

And if they did make cowboy shows again with the old innocence, how would they portray the bad guys? Would today's audience buy in to evil business tycoons without violence? Losing the ranch because of big business corruption might have too much real emotional connection to today's audience. We've lived it and seen it up close and personal, and we had no stranger ride into town to save the day.

How does your business fit into the old west analogy? Do your company's business practices compare to the wicked land barons, railroads, bankers, or any of the outlaw gangs whose objective was all about amassing wealth and power? And in doing so, cared nothing about the people who were losing their land and livelihood. Or is your company more like one with a mission to bring peace and prosperity for all, build communities with schools, shops and infrastructure?

What about your role. If your company is one of the good guys, are you doing your part to support the mission, participate in civic and charity events, develop and grow your people so they can share in the good fortune?

What if your company is one of the bad guys? Do you do enough to challenge the business purpose and ethics you know are wrong? Do you do all you can to stop the mistreatment of employees or customers? You may think that is out of your level or area of responsibility. We will learn later in this book that you are indeed empowered to speak your voice when you find matters unethical or illegal. And if you are powerless to influence change, do you have the courage to blow the whistle and stand up for what is right? What you may view as a terrible career move may prove to be just that. But like our heroes from the old west, it may be the proper life move. Doing the right thing usually comes out on top over the long term; doing nothing may dodge a bullet for the short term, but you could end up going down with the bad guys.

One of my consulting clients was a high-tech company that was engaged in a highly unethical and illegal activity. Their business produced a large volume of hazardous waste as a byproduct. It was very expensive to properly dispose of this waste. So they used proper practices for only a small amount of the waste so as not to raise suspicion. The major portion was put in metal drums. They had rented warehouse space across town for storage. The drums of hazardous waste were trucked to the warehouse, where the contents were simply poured down the drains. Except for the three or four workers who were performing the operation, the rest of the workforce had no idea of this practice. Nor did I.

Eventually they got caught. The husband and wife who owned the business were fined several million dollars and the husband served jail time. The company eventually folded. To my amazement, instead of being outraged, many employees stood by in support of the owners. A number attended the trial and spoke on their behalf. I was in disbelief. These people operated their business illegally, used unfair business practices, and were destroying the environment. I lost a client, but approximately 300 employees lost their jobs and a large number of them still supported the owners. What happened to their sense of right and wrong? Bring back the values of the old west.

Chapter 3

Values lost in business & politics

"Try not to become a man of success, but rather try to become a man of value."- Albert Einstein

Joe Ehrmann played football at Syracuse University, and in the NFL for the Baltimore Colts and Detroit Lions. He then became an ordained minister, and volunteer football coach at Gilman High School in Maryland. He has won numerous civic awards and recognitions. He became famous because he taught his players values of life; such as "athletic ability, sexual conquest and economic success are not the best measurements of manhood," "build and value relationships," "practice the concepts of empathy, inclusion and integrity," just to quote a few. This man is a genuine local hero, who knows the most important thing we can teach our children are values. Never mind that his team had a great won-lost record, several undefeated seasons, and won the state championship – he wanted to leave behind much more than that with his student-athletes. Joe and his wife Paula founded an organization called Coach for America. Here is the Coach for America mission statement: "To inform, inspire and initiate individual, communal and societal change that will empower men and women to be their very best – personally, professionally and relationally."

Which brings to mind the many local heroes we have who we can use as positive examples in teaching our children life's basic values – fair and equal treatment of people, knowing and choosing right from wrong. There are many teachers, coaches and parents who have served to inspire young people though their mentoring, and leading by example. Many of these people have no formal leadership training; and most go unrecognized for their contributions. Yet, we all owe them an enormous amount of gratitude. We have high expectations, even demands, that they be held to the highest standards with their own behavior and relay these positive influences on our children, who we place in their hands.

I feel I have been blessed with a good sense of values, which I try to use when making decisions and conducting my daily activities. To whom do I owe these values? My family, many teachers, members of the clergy, and various coworkers, bosses and business leaders over the years. All on the local level. I also know many local business leaders, company owners, general managers; people I am proud to know and work with, who earn and deserve tremendous admiration and respect from their employees and the community in which they serve.

Unfortunately, it sometimes happens that when people called Leaders get on a larger stage, their values, as well as the public's expectations of their values, go in an inverse proportion. If you are a member of a major corporation with a senior management team that places employee appreciation and customer values above personal wealth, power, ego and ambition – applaud them, for you may be in rare company. I personally worked in two large corporations where I saw firsthand the level of corruption and greed, illegal and unethical activities, right in line with what came to light at the time in the Enron, Global Crossing, and Tyco scandals. I was a Vice President of Human Resources for a major corporation when I was told, by my President, that I must learn how to more effectively play company politics. My response was that my role was not to play company politics, but to uphold values. We both got what we wanted. He got to become a millionaire, and I got to pursue my career elsewhere. Are these evil people? Not necessarily, but they use a different set of standards in the performance of their jobs, than when raising their own children. They feel an action, although it may defy mission statement values, is still proper if justified as a business decision. Values overruled, that's business.

Which leads to the ultimate position of leadership – the President of the United States. President Bill Clinton was involved in a sex scandal which could have, should have, and would have gotten any worker fired, justifiably, from any business enterprise. Having sex on company time, on company premises – fired, case closed. Then our next President, George Bush, took the country into a war under questionable intelligence, at a cost of thousands of lives and trillions of dollars. Again, such a blunder would get any business manager removed. I say any manager, not necessarily any CEO or President. Why? Because we don't hold our top leaders to the high value standards which we hold our teachers, coaches, ministers, or even parents. A sex or financial scandal would get you removed from a position of little league coach, head of a church committee, or running the bake sale for the Parent Teachers Association. In those positions, we have expectations of high ethical and moral values; but it's not quite as accountable in major corporate or government leadership.

Presidential and congressional elections typically run an intentional campaign of discrediting the opponent's reputation. In sports we call this "trash talk." A prominent political strategist stated on a talk show, with pride, that the campaign is working well – it is keeping the focus off the issues not favoring my candidate; while questioning the opponent's reputation, whether factual or not. What an insult to us citizens! When other countries do this, we call it propaganda, and it's bad. When we do it, we call it spin, and its clever strategy. No negatives towards the opponent are tolerated in youth sports; but on the political grand stage – anything goes. Values overruled, that's politics.

In sports, through all the major professional leagues, we see talented athletes involved in drugs, shootings, domestic violence and cheating scandals. Why is it so many people are unsupportive and without sympathy, stating they were glad those sports figures got punished? Because the athletes we had admired as role models turned out to be arrogant, overpaid, uncompassionate and selfish individuals. We as a people won't accept that from our sports figures – but we tolerate it from our business and government leaders!

Going back to the expression "all is fair in love and war." What a silly myth. There are many things unfair, unacceptable, unethical, dishonorable, despicable, and even criminal, in love and war; as there are in business and politics; as there are in life. Let's teach our children true values of fair and equal treatment of all people; building and maintaining healthy and positive relationships; helping those in need, and honoring those we should. Let's recognize the positive contributions of our own local heroes – teachers, clergy, coaches, police, firefighters, other public servants, business leaders, and parents. As today's children become tomorrow's leaders, we must impact them with the bottom-line ethical judgment of what's right from what's wrong – and make that value system immune to the excuse of "that's business, that's politics."

A lot of guilt can be written off when we tell ourselves, "This was a tough business decision." I've heard executives say they do not want to know things about an employee's personal life because they don't want any emotions to affect their judgement. They pride themselves as being hard and cold when running their business. Yet they want public recognition for being a good model citizen, and leader of a company who contributes to the community.

How do they get so mislead? I often wonder how they can turn the switch to be normal, outgoing, happy people among their own family and friends. Maybe they don't. But I do know that the most admired and respected leaders I have observed are down-to-earth, friendly men and women. They are not afraid to talk with people at all levels, and share their outside interests and activities. Something as simple as "How's your daughter enjoying college?" might lift that person's day, and make you sound more human. Yet we have some managers who would never do that sort of thing. They prefer to intimidate people, remain standoffish, and avoid personal relationships.

Which type would you rather have for a role model? Which type would you give extra effort for, do what you can to help them succeed and look good? Of course, the person you like, which is the person who shows that they care about you.

And when you are that right kind of leader, one who is not afraid of your own emotions; you build and maintain friendly and trusting relationships with employees, peers, customers and business partners. You know you can still make the business and people decisions when required. In fact, they may be easier, not more difficult. The most successful managers at every level are those who are comfortable with being themselves, and don't try to alter their own personality to fit some image they have of a boss.

Chapter 4

The Fall of my Heroes

"Oh, somewhere in this favored land
the sun is shining bright.
The band is playing somewhere,
and somewhere hearts are light.
And somewhere men are laughing,
and somewhere children shout.
But there is no joy in Mudville.
Mighty Casey has struck out."
- Ernest Lawrence Thayer

The quote above is the last verse of the famous poem Casey at the Bat. A poem which remains popular more than 125 years after it was written, and has been made into numerous children's books, a cartoon movie, a silent movie, thousands of reprinting's and comedy skits. One famous vaudeville comedian, DeWolf Hopper, made a living by doing a Casey at the Bat stage act for several decades. It is believed he performed the act over 10,000 times. Baseball Almanac dubbed it the single most famous baseball poem ever written.

Truly, the poem is a comedy classic. The thirteen verses are all written about a baseball game featuring the hometown heroes, the

Mudville Nine. The story starts in the bottom of the ninth inning with Mudville trailing 4 to 2. And in the first verse the first two batters, Cooney and Burrows, both got outs. Now we're two down, two runs behind, and only our hero Casey could save the day; but we had no chance since the next two guys up were Flynn and Blake, who as the poem states, Flynn was pudding and Blake was a fake. Then like a miracle, Flynn hit a single followed by Blake's double. Suddenly we had runners on second and third, and the winning run comes to the plate, none other than our famous slugger Casey. The 5,000 fans went wild. Casey smiled and doffed his hat, the stage was set for the home team victory. Casey didn't like the first two pitches, which were called strikes. The crowd roared, someone yelled "kill the umpire," but no one was really worried. It just built the suspense for the ultimate heroics, the storybook ending. Then came the world famous, ultimately disappointing, and unbelievably anti-climactic, swing-and-a-miss. The mighty Casey had struck out.

The fallen hero in the story is of course Casey. But there is also a very interesting story about the person who penned this marvelous poem. The author of Casey at the Bat was Ernest Lawrence Thayer. Ernest was born into wealth and privilege in 1863 in Massachusetts, where his father owned several woolen mills. Highly intelligent, Ernest went to Harvard, where he graduated magna cum laude as a Philosophy major. His goal was to be a writer and lecturer of philosophy. While at Harvard he was an editor of the Harvard Lampoon and a member of the Hasty Pudding theatrical club, both noted institutions that are still prestigious today. A good friend, classmate, and fellow member of both the Lampoon and Hasty Pudding, was the later world renowned William Randolph Hearst. After graduation, Hearst convinced Ernest to come to San Francisco and write for him at the San Francisco Examiner. He wrote mostly editorials and advertisement copy, using his real name or initials. Occasionally he would write a comic piece, for which he would use the pseudonym Phin, his penname from the Harvard Lampoon. In 1888, at age 24, he wrote Casey at the Bat, and it was printed in the paper. He moved on from that job, but some people had seen the poem in the paper, cut it out and kept it, and eventually its popularity began to grow. A success story indeed, and fame and wealth were sure to follow.

Over the years the poem was recited, printed, and acted out; and many people made money doing so. However, Ernest Thayer never received any royalty – he didn't want to. There were even imposters claiming they were Phin, the author, but the Hearst organization had proof that it belonged to Ernest Thayer. Instead of Casey at the Bat becoming his road to fame and fortune, he allowed it to become his curse. He simply did not want to be known as a comedy writer, and said the poem was of little quality and caused him annoyance and disgust. He wanted to be known as a serious writer and philosopher. He moved to Europe for a while to travel and work. Unfortunately, for the rest of his life he never achieved the recognition he desired as a serious author and lecturer. He created something that gave pleasure to thousands, yet it gave no satisfaction to himself. Ernest, like the character Casey, was disappointed in his own outcome. And the outcome broke the hearts of the fans who adored them.

BENJAMIN ZANDER

"Never doubt the capacity of the people you lead to accomplish whatever you are dreaming." - Benjamin Zander

Ben Zander was born in England in 1939, and was musically gifted. He began to compose music at the age of nine. His main instrument was the cello, and as a youth studied under famous cellists and attended prestigious music academies in England, Italy and Germany. He traveled throughout Europe playing with orchestras, performing concerts, and studying. He obtained a degree in English Literature. In the mid 1960's he came to the United States for graduate work at Brandeis and Harvard Universities.

He became a professor at the New England Conservatory, a world renowned school for gifted musicians; and also founded the Boston Philharmonic Orchestra. He continued to travel and make appearances as a guest conductor for some of the world's finest adult and youth symphony orchestras.

I became aware of Ben Zander, and intrigued by his accomplishments several years ago when I saw a leadership video he made called The Art of Possibility. The video is taken from a book by the same title written by Ben and Rosamund Zander. Ben's wife,

Rosamund Stone Zander, is a psychologist, family therapist and executive coach. She observed how he would take people who were already gifted and talented, and make them even better. After all, you had to audition and be selected to enter the New England Conservatory, and you were competing with elite musicians from all over the world. Likewise, any person joining a symphony orchestra had to already be an accomplished musician. His job was to then take them to an even higher level. Rosamund studied how he went about doing this – the processes and guidelines he followed, and how he inspired and encouraged his students. Together, they conceptualized the theory he had in motivating people and formulized a set of key principles:

Speak and think in terms of "possibilities." Not hard set goals, rather more like dreams and aspirations - identify levels of attainment that just might be possible.

Recognize the downward spiral. Be aware when negative influences in your life are pulling you in that direction and stop it.

Enroll other people in your journey. You are not in any venture alone. Recognize your support team, encourage and involve them in your journey.

Lead by making others more powerful. Don't let your own ego demand that you get all the credit and maintain all the control; rather, take pride in the development and achievements of your team, and enable them to gain the recognition.

Lead from any chair. Regardless of your position, place or title, you have the personal accountability to speak up and do the right thing. And if the right thing is to challenge those above you, it is your responsibility to do so.

Enroll every voice in the vision. That means it is everyone's job, not just the leader, to encourage and include participation from every member of the team.

Look for shining eyes. Find the people who are already engaged, motivated, giving their all and enjoying their role. These are the people you want to align with for your own happiness and success.

Quiet the voice in the head. The voice that tells you that you can't do it. You can be your own worst critic, and talk yourself right out of the challenge.

Everybody gets an A. This one needs further explanation because it is so intriguing. When Ben started teaching at the New England Conservatory he noticed how many students were intimidated by their peers, and there was so much pressure to meet the high standards that were before them. They were of course worried about their grades. Ben wanted them to focus on achieving a higher level of performance than they had ever achieved, and that meant taking risks. So in order to remove the pressure, he told them that just to be there, they were already among the very best in their abilities. Thus, they were already "A" students. On the first day of class, he announces that everyone's final grade will be an A. Everybody gets an A. It changed the whole learning atmosphere. There was no longer competitiveness, but rather a sense of family, where they all encouraged and brought out the best in each other. And all they had to do to earn that A, was at the end of the semester, submit a paper to Ben that starts with "I got my A because…" Over the years he has received many amazing papers, and most do not even pertain to music. They go on to state how this class has changed their life as a person, and how they have overcame their fears. The concept of the A is truly inspirational, and can be adapted to the level of expectations for any team.

Give people a possibility to live into, not an expectation to live up to. This is my personal favorite. The whole point of Art of Possibility is to inspire creativity, out-of-.the-box thinking. So you must encourage them to achieve their dreams. Do not set a defined goal whereby attaining it is either passing or failing, winning or losing – that way the focus is on the score or the grade, not on the accomplishment.

Remember rule #6! When asked, rule number 6 is "Don't take yourself so damn seriously." Keep a humility; no one is perfect all the time; no one is great the first time; no one knows it all or is expected to know it all. And without humor, what good is any undertaking. When people respond that is a great rule, and ask what the other rules are, the answer is "there are no other rules, only rule #6."

So for years Ben and Rose Zander inspired thousands of people, both in live seminars and through their book and video production, The Art of Possibility. They were in demand around the world for seminar and coaching engagements, as well as serving as a guest conductor for some of the world's finest symphony orchestras. Ben would combine his classes at the New England Conservatory with his leadership seminars and have students perform in their programs, and relate their stories of how they reached a higher level of performance, and more meaning to how they were living their lives, through Ben Zander's inspiration.

I was inspired as well. I purchased the video and cases of the book, and did research on the Zanders' fascinating background. I put together a power point presentation to prep my audience for the video. The Art of Possibility is still a key part of the leadership development programs at our company, and we give every participant a copy of the book. It is very effective and always a favorite segment of our program.

The fall: In January of 2012 Ben Zander was fired from the New England Conservatory after serving on their staff for 45 years, and bringing so much acclaim to the institution. The reason for the firing was that Ben had hired a videographer to film student concerts and rehearsals – ten years earlier. Turns out the videographer had committed crimes of sexually abusing teenagers, more than 20 years earlier. The offender had undergone a rigorous rehabilitation program and served prison time, and had no further incidents since all this had occurred in the 1990's. Plus he was an employee of the school, not of Ben Zander, and did work for other departments in addition to Zander's classes. It was the school's role to conduct the necessary background checks for any employee. But in only a few short weeks since the matter was uncovered, following their "investigation," the school fired Ben Zander.

JOSEPH VINCENT PATERNO

"What counts in sports is not the victory, but the magnificence of the struggle." - Joe Paterno

Joe Paterno was born and raised in Brooklyn, New York. He and his brother George played football together at Brown University, where they graduated in 1950. Joe's goal was to become a lawyer, but he went with Coach Rip Engle, who was leaving Brown to take on the head coaching position at Penn State University. He thought he would help his mentor as an assistant coach before entering law school.

The rest is history. Joe was a member of the Penn State coaching staff for the next 62 years. He served as head coach for 46 years, the longest serving head coach at one school in the history of college football. His 409 wins make him the winningest coach in FBS history. His teams appeared in 37 bowl games, and won 24. There have been books written about his records and achievements, far too many to mention here. But the statistic he was most proud of is that 87% of his players graduated. He and his wife Sue have donated more than $4 million to the university. And the building that bears his name is not the football stadium, but the library.

Joe ran a program with the motto "Success with Honor," which meant he ran a clean program and always showed respect to the school, the fans, and the opponent. And when he took over as head coach he implemented something called "The Grand Experiment" which challenged all athletes to excel both on the field and in the classroom. He always reminded the student-athletes that they were students first, and were there to get a fine education. It is said that he didn't recruit the athletes as much as he recruited their parents, promising them that their sons would attend classes and earn a degree. He encouraged them to use this opportunity to select a worthy field of study as their major, which would carry them to their future success. "JoePa" was loved and respected by millions of people – former players, students, alumni, fans, and opposing players and coaches. Penn State was a model as a fine academic institution with an unblemished record for athletic improprieties.

The fall: In early November of 2011 Jerry Sandusky was arrested on charges of child sexual abuse. Four days later Joe Paterno was fired from Penn State University. The official reason, released four months later by the Board of Trustees, was for "failure of leadership." When the Pennsylvania State Attorney General announced the arrest of Jerry Sandusky, she also announced that the university President, Vice President, and Athletic Director were also under investigation. In that announcement she specifically stated that head football coach Joe Paterno is not accused of any wrongdoing.

In 1998 the Centre County District Attorney investigated similar charges against Sandusky and decided that no criminal charges were warranted. In 1999 Sandusky retired from Penn State and the football program. However he was still permitted to use an office and facilities, in part to support his role as Director of The Second Mile, a charity organization. In 2002 Paterno was advised of improper conduct between Sandusky and a small boy. The next day Paterno reported this information to his superiors, who informed him this would be dealt with as a police matter.

Ten years after the incident occurred, and more than six months after Paterno was fired, the NCAA implemented unprecedented and illogical punishments to the university and its football program. Sandusky was eventually found guilty on 45 counts of sexual misconduct, and sentenced 30 to 60 years in prison. But the man whose legacy and lifetime of honorable achievements were tarnished was Joe Paterno.

———————————

Many similarities can be drawn between the events of Ben Zander and Joe Paterno. Indeed, their firings from their fine institutions happened within two months of each other. Many believe that the New England Conservatory took such swift action against Zander as a result of the media circus that surrounded the similar situation at Penn State, which was still going on. Joe Paterno died from cancer on January 22, just ten days after Ben Zander was fired.

Both were situations involving sexual misconduct with children, an unforgiving and disgusting behavior, which no one acknowledges as acceptable. And in both cases, the responsible person received proper legal trial and punishment. Neither Zander nor Paterno in any way condoned such behavior, and most important – neither orchestrated a cover up.

Yet both were found by many in the public to be guilty by association. And in both cases, the administrations of otherwise fine and respectable educational institutions, rushed to judgement in light of media pressure, with insufficient investigation of the facts.

Ben Zander and Joe Paterno were both super popular with their musicians/players, and throughout the student body. Both considered themselves teachers and wanted to mold their students for life beyond their music or football. Both had millions of fans and admirers.

We all have heroes – people we admire, want to emulate, and use as a role model. And trust me – your children do – you are probably one of their trusted heroes. We are loyal fans; we accept our hero's mistakes. After all, they're human – nobody's perfect. They, like us, are vulnerable. Anyone can easily become a victim of life's circumstances. When a hero falls, we question our loyalty, we question our judgement.

Your fallen hero might be your boss, or your company President. Many a person has walked into work on a given morning to find that their admired role model has "left to pursue other interests." Just like that your pleasant, secure work environment is shattered.

On a large stage like New England Conservatory or Penn State University we cannot do too much other than be a voice in the crowd. We can write letters and emails, and that's not to be downplayed. Thousands of voices do make an impact.

But when it's local – in your company, church, school or community – it is your duty and responsibility to speak up for what is right. We live in a world that is often cruel, unjust and violent. We must do all we can to help law enforcement solve crimes, take perpetrators off the street, and make our neighborhoods safer. I think we all agree on that.

However, what is often more difficult is the refusal to remain silent. Do we see wrongdoing and say nothing because we don't want to get involved? Do we speak up for people who are wrongly accused? Do we question someone getting fired when the punishment far exceeds the crime – when others have done worse with no similar discipline?

We cannot respect ourselves and our companies if we look the other way and remain silent, and allow injustice. One day we, or someone in our family, might be the innocent victim who is disgraced by another person's actions. Do not remain silent when you see wrongdoing. A motto I often quote, "It never hurts to do the right thing."

Chapter 5

Defined by your work

"Nobody on their deathbed has ever said they wished they would have spent more time at the office." - Rabbi Harold Kushner

It started when we were little kids and people would ask "What do you want to be when you grow up?" At any age you were expected to have an answer, and it had better be something glamorous. Say the wrong thing and your parents would die of embarrassment. And as you got older it had to be something worthy, dignified, and realistically attainable. Yet I never heard any child answer "I'd like to obtain an entry level opportunity with an established company and grow into a career in middle management." Would that answer have made your father proud, or would that have gotten you sent off to military school?

Now it never fails, whenever people meet someone new, one of the first questions is "What do you do?" If you are the parent of a teenager, and they tell you about a new friend or date, do you ask "What do their parents do?" Think of the stigma we all place on someone's place of work, type of business, and job title. Work defines our status in society, and it is how other people judge us and how we judge other people.

Maybe it should. After all, our work generally determines where we live, how we live, what we can afford to do for fun, and if we will have time for fun. Most people from their early 20's to their mid or late 60's, will spend more hours per average week working than they will spend sleeping, eating, recreation, education, or family activities. Work defines our life because it is so much of our life. It is absolutely necessary if we want to eat and buy things, or at least keep us out of boredom and poverty. So we might as well enjoy it and reap the benefits it provides.

So kids, you better be very careful about choosing what you want to do for a living, becausve what you do is what you'll become. No pressure there. And then there is the moment in life when some people lose their job. That can have disastrous effects, you have lost your purpose. It can be devastating emotionally, in addition to losing salary and benefits. Some people even feel a sense of shame and may suffer depression.

SOME PEOPLE LOVE THEIR JOB

> *"Choose a job you love, and you will never have to work a day in your life." - Confucius*

Let's start with people who really enjoy their work. Yes, many people do. Hopefully, most people do. Renee Weisman did research to determine why some people really love their job.

The biggest factor was the challenge of their work. People who love their job, love the challenge of it. It gives them the opportunity to apply their skills and creativity to solve problems. It's like you cross a threshold in your career when you realize you are no longer paid for your time or even your work output, but now you are paid for your brain. Challenges arise when work presents change and variety. Happy people at work do not like the mundane, they want to continually learn and experience new challenges.

The next reason was attributed to a great boss. A great boss can be motivating, inspiring, and allow people to pursue the challenge without being directed through every step. A great boss gives people freedom to think and develop ideas, and recognizes them for their accomplishments.

The third factor was of course great coworkers. People want to enjoy the people they are around throughout the day, but also share in the challenges and collaborate as a team. People want to respect their coworkers as talented and caring.

A fourth factor had to do with the purpose and mission of the company – work that matters. People want to make a difference in improving something for somebody. We may not all have the opportunity to impact the world, but there is great satisfaction in helping others or achieving a worthy goal.

The final major factor was just being grateful for having a good job. People have grown to appreciate a safe job with a stable organization, after seeing so much turbulence in the job market for a number of years.

Interestingly, there were some comments in the survey around flexibility and work/life balance, but not a single respondent stated salary or benefits as a prime reason for loving their job.

So people who love their job are probably happy to be defined by it. They may ask others what they do, in hopes that they will be asked in return. Then they can go on to talk about their favorite subject, their contribution to a worthy purpose, with wonderful people, and having the freedom to apply their talents and contribute.

SOME PEOPLE HATE THEIR JOB

"If you don't like your job you don't strike. You just go in every day and do it really half-assed. That's the American way." - Homer Simpson

Even if you are lucky enough to have a decent paying job, you may not be very excited to get up and go to work in the morning, don't feel much appreciated while you're there, find it difficult to get much accomplished, aren't having much rewarding socialization through the day, and don't see where what you are doing makes much of a difference anyway.

Numerous studies have been done on employee engagement, and most show quite similar results. A Gallup study showed that just 30% of employees in America feel actively engaged at work. That means really love what they do, feel loyalty to the organization, and no chance of leaving. Only 30%! How effective is your team with only 30% gun-ho engagement?

By contrast, 20% of the people were shown to be actively disengaged. That means outward negativity. They hate the place, hate even being there. Furthermore, the active part of their disengagement is to convince coworkers that this is a terrible place, horrible boss, greedy senior management, horrendous working environment, and so on – and we should all leave or at least not give much of an effort. We'll make management look bad, that's our purpose.

The remaining 50% are kind of lukewarm mediocre. The job's ok, it's a job. It's too much effort to look for another job, and it would probably just be the same thing. There are some good days, and they treat us alright. I'll just do what I'm told, and run out the clock until I retire. I'm not that much into work anyway, it's just a paycheck. Pays the bills.

So where should we put our effort? It seems pretty simple by design. Reward and encourage the top 30%, and let's focus on the in-between 50% and try to inspire and motivate them. Surely, we can get a majority of them to move up the scale. As for the negative 20%, get rid of them. They are destructive to our organization, and maybe they will find somewhere else they may enjoy a little more.

Unfortunately, the reality is often that the disengaged 20% burns out the management's time and energy, while spreading their venom to those in the vulnerable 50%.

Going back to the Weisman study, she also surveyed the people who hate their jobs, and the number one reason she found was that the job is boring. Many felt their work was menial, was repetitive, or did not yield results. So if we can correct those perceptions, maybe there is hope in converting people from job haters into job lovers. We should be able to make any job more fun and interesting.

Not surprisingly, the number two reason was having a bad boss. We often hear the expression, "people don't quit the company, they quit their boss." Well, it is very true. Too many people are unqualified to supervise others, and likely have never undergone real management training, or do not continue management training on an ongoing basis. They may come across as too strong, too weak, uninterested, uninvolved, or take all the credit. Of course their people are going to be unhappy.

The third reason was lack of personal time. You as a leader may be a workaholic, and proud of it, but don't demand or expect that your people should be. People want to work hard and do a good job; but they also want a life and some flexibility in meeting family obligations.

The fourth reason was a miserable working environment. People enjoy working as a team, and want to feel a part of the team. However, too often management ignores the team dynamic and allows certain people to feel totally left out, thus creating a difficult and unfriendly environment.

The number five reason was poor pay. While pay was not a major factor in why people love their job, it certainly came into play why people hate their job. When people feel underpaid they feel underappreciated.

If you are in the "hate my job" category, is there any hope? Fortunately there is. Question yourself as to why – it may be a combination of several factors. If you find the work boring, try to change that. You may be in a menial, repetitive job because you need a skill set to move to more challenging work. Determine what that is and seek available training, coursework or online classes, mentoring. Let your desires become known that you want to grow your skills and experience.

If the problem is your boss, try to repair the relationship. Prove yourself by showing that you can handle the job and obtain results with a positive attitude. That may be your biggest challenge – you must feel and display a consistent positive attitude. Your boss may be just as frustrated with his or her job, and the two of you may be able to focus on some productive changes.

Is there any room for compromise with more personal time? This varies by industry and job function. Some occupations are by nature very adaptable to working on your own, from any location.

Some just cannot find the flexibility due to the schedule, type of work, or coordination with teams. If this is an absolute for you, then ask yourself if you need to change occupations. Or is it just a temporary thing? For example, tax accountants know they will have little free time from mid-January through mid-April. They also know things will get better after tax season. Doctors know through their residency they will work extremely demanding schedules, but again that will be temporary to a better life beyond that period. Many projects require long hours to meet a deadline, but there will be some bonus recovery time when the project ends.

STARTING YOUR OWN BUSINESS

"I freed a thousand slaves. I could have saved a thousand more if only they knew they were slaves." - Harriet Tubman

Some people are born entrepreneurs and wouldn't think of working for someone else. They like to own things, and be in control. The world is full of successful people doing just that. Some of them make good leaders, some do not.

Most people would not be comfortable taking the risk to start their own business, then wondering each day if there will be enough business the next day. They prefer the security of a regular job with a regular paycheck and someone else taking the risk.

As we have seen through various economic times, neither scenario guarantees safety and security. The same dynamics of loving or hating your job can apply, no matter if you work in a large company, a small business, or your own business.

Rickey Gold wrote an interesting article titled "The 7 Perils of Entrepreneurship." Most perils are not foreseen as people venture into their own business.

Peril 1. Time Mismanagement. It's easy to fall into a life without scheduled hours. In fact, you may start living without a schedule at all. But your business will become your life, and you may find you are spending all of your time working. Customers know that an established business has scheduled hours, but they may expect you to be there for them 24/7. When watching a television show in the evening without a computer on your lap gives you a guilty feeling, you know you have lost control of your time.

Peril 2. Organizational Skills. Usually the lack thereof. Maybe you didn't count on the records, receipts, licenses, or the other multitude of paperwork. If you didn't like bookkeeping, reporting and filing before, do you think you will enjoy it now? How about ordering and paying for supplies, right down to the paper clips. I've heard it said that once you're self-employed, a paper clip never hits the floor. Because you have to purchase the replacement.

Peril 3. Focus, or lack of. You may have thoroughly loved doing your thing when it was your hobby, and never seemed to have enough time for it. Now it has become a job, and not as much fun when people are paying for it, because they are much more critical. And they give you a deadline of when they expect it. Remember, you are your own boss, and you are in control. Maybe not so much. Do you still want to do it all the time?

Other people starting a business may tell themselves, now I can make my own schedule, do more activities with the kids, get involved at school, read books, take vacations, go shopping or see a movie during the week. Ok, so who's going to run the business? When?

Peril 4. Fear of Failure. Entrepreneurship means taking risks, which means stretching your abilities, taking chances, maybe overcommitting, maybe going without appropriate legal advice. Most successful entrepreneurs not only have stories of failures, they are usually proud to talk and laugh about them. They know that's part of being an entrepreneur. Can you handle that?

Peril 5. Lack of Marketing. I've known so many small business owners who said they love doing the work, which is usually why they started the business. However, they are not spending their time doing the work now, they are spending their time networking and selling. Which in many cases is the part they dislike, and the part they are not good at. Plus, it is very easy to throw money at costly advertising which may be the wrong venue, doesn't reach the audience you need, and doesn't bring you any business. I knew two partners who started a small business venture and failed. I asked them if they could have done things differently. One answered "Yes, but we wouldn't have at the time. If we would have had another $10,000 or $20,000, we would have spent it all on more advertising, which did not bring us any business." There are a lot of sales people in advertising and marketing companies who will be more than happy to help you spend your money.

Peril 6. Not Staying on Top of Your Game. Seminars were an expense and time consumer when you worked for an employer, but kept your knowledge on the leading edge. Now you don't have the time or budget to spend on continuing your learning curve.

Peril 7. Forgetting to Have Fun. This is a very impactful one, especially if you have a family. You may have gotten into this with full family support, because you were convinced you would be doing what you loved. Now you are afraid to take a day off. You can remember complaining that you only got three weeks of vacation at the company, but now you haven't taken a single day off in the past year.

And as for not having a boss, you may have customers who become more demanding than your boss ever was. You no longer have other people serving as buffers or taking the blame – you are the complaint department.

I'm not trying to discourage anyone from starting a business. Indeed, it can be the most rewarding and satisfying thing you ever did. You are your own boss, you are in control, you are doing what you love and making the best use of your talent. The key is to have total awareness and thoroughly plan each phase. Stay flexible. You may have to make major changes if things go too slow – you need more credit, you need to expand product lines, you need a different marketing approach. Or it can also be a problem if things go too good too fast – you have to work longer hours, maybe outsource or hire people. That's what gives many successful business owners the rush – making decisions on your own and acting fast. No bureaucracy, no red tape, no upper management presentations or approval necessary. You just do it!

HR FOR HIRE, INC.

I grew up in the small town of Neffs, Pennsylvania. My father was a small business owner. Laman CG Snyder Floor Coverings of

Neffs. They did carpeting, vinyl flooring, floor tile, ceramic tile, countertops. He usually had four employees. Four guys, two trucks, and he did all the estimating, purchasing and scheduling. Mother did the bookkeeping. He did a lot of marketing and advertising because he loved that part. Throughout the local area, most everybody knew him. He was a real entrepreneur and loved it, wouldn't have been happy doing anything else. But a professional businessman he was not. He also worked seven-day weeks, and was out most evenings. I saw how hard he worked and the problems he had, and I was convinced I never wanted to own my own business.

After I graduated college and joined the working world, my thought was the bigger the company, the better. Bigger companies would have more opportunities. Frankly, things were working out in that regard. I had good positions and opportunities to learn and grow with Restaura, a part of the Greyhound Dial Corporation; and with Steelcase. Both very large international corporations. Then followed a short stint with a horrible company, which I will write about later. That bad experience led me to my next venture, which was starting a business.

The thing I swore I would never do. Suddenly, the desire hit me. I wanted to start a business. What would I do? How would I do it? First of all, I did not take the road that many take, which is to get into something they know nothing about. People will start a small restaurant, a pizza shop, a print shop, a dry cleaners, a sign shop, or any of a multitude of things, often through a franchise. Sounds easy, you invest, they train you, and they will advertise and generate customers for you. All you have to do is commit to adhere to their standards, and give them an up-front franchise fee, and a percentage of your revenues. I don't mean to downplay this. Many people have become wealthy, happy, and even grown this arrangement into owning multiple stores. But it wasn't what I had in mind.

What I knew and enjoyed was Human Resources. I did some research and saw that back in my hometown region there were numerous small businesses of all types with a range of 25 to 200 employees. I figured a lot of them had no human resources support. Sure enough I was right. I talked to many business owners who would say things like

"I have 50 employees. I'm not big enough to have a Human Resources Manager, but I have 50 problems every month." Music to my ears.

Thus, I decided to open a consulting business called HR For HIRE. If we learn from our mistakes, I'll share some of mine so you can learn from things I did wrong. First, although I was moving back to my home area, I had been away for almost 15 years, and didn't have a single business contact there. Second, blame me for being a visionary, my vision was having a nice office and facility, not starting out of a briefcase and growing something. So the first thing I did was rent 2000 feet of office space, furnish it with new and beautiful furniture. I had a swanky office, a nice reception area, a classroom for running meetings and training, 20 work stations with panels and phones plus a library for a job placement center. Then before I did anything I ordered printed letterhead, stationary, business cards and brochures. I purchased a phone system, computers, printers, and fax machine. I hired a receptionist to greet people and do all our typing and printing. Now I had a great place to open my doors for business. All I needed were customers. Did you ever hear the expression, built it and they will come? Didn't happen. Where did I get all the money to do this? We sold our home and rented a townhouse in order to stake this venture. I convinced my wife Denise this will be a great investment in our future. Denise was already self-employed as an interior designer.

The first few years were really a grind. I was making calls for hours every day to try to get appointments to see business owners or human resources representatives. I was calling on companies of all sizes. Fortunately, I got a few assignments, just enough to keep us breaking even. Although not making much of a profit, we at least didn't lose any money. I would get some outplacement business from large companies, wrote a lot of employee handbooks and conducted a lot of human resource audits for middle size companies, and did some hiring and handled personnel issues for small companies.

Then I got lucky. My networking was starting to pay off. The phone started ringing, and business owners would say I need your help with something. I started to get companies on retainer, where we ran their human resources function. A few large employers asked us to do training or assessment work.

I was asked to be a member of the Board of Directors for the Small Business Council of the Greater Lehigh Valley Chamber of Commerce. A Chamber which was on an aggressive growth mode through acquisition, and grew into one of the largest Chamber organizations in the country. I was on the Board for eight years and served as President of the Small Business Council for two. This gave me and my business a great deal of exposure, and I built many valuable relationships.

We had clients in almost every type of business imaginable. We had retainer customers in construction, a chemical company, a meat company, and a plastics company. We had a large real estate company and an insurance company, a bank, and a high-tech company. We had non-profits such as a charity, an eye bank, a rescue mission, and several churches. We had public sector businesses in three townships and a school district.

We moved out of our rented office space and purchased our own office building, which Denise redesigned and remodeled. It had good highway frontage and signage, and housed our business, plus we rented out office space to other small businesses.

There we were. Owning two businesses plus a commercial property. Both being our own boss. And after the early struggle, which even meant going without health insurance for a while, we were back on our feet. We were able to once again purchase a home, and put our son through college. It was a rewarding experience, but very challenging. Owning you own business means providing your own insurance, funding your own retirement plan or not having one, paying both halves of social security contributions, providing your own office supplies, and numerous other elements taken for granted when you work for a company.

In addition to outsourcing the human resources department, a big part of HR For HIRE was also running a job search center. When I opened the business I decided that no matter what my financial situation, all personal friends, relatives, and anyone in the human resources family would receive our services at no cost. So anyone in those categories got free resume service and free use our facilities. I would make calls and network for them. We ran routine seminars on how to network, job search, interview, negotiate, and they were always welcomed and encouraged to participate, again at no cost. We even ran a program called the Human Resources Job Bank, which was a free resource where any business or search firm could post any open human resources position, and any person could post their resume. We made many successful matches. Helping people who are out of work is a practice I still do to this day. I have helped many people get new jobs, and I find nothing more personally satisfying than that.

So how did I do with the perils? Time management, organization skills, focus, staying on top of game – check, check, check, check. Did pretty well with those. Fear of failure, that was a tough one. No matter how busy I was and no matter how happy my clients seemed to be, I always worried about future business. Will our clients stay loyal, will the business continue to grow? This is what kept me up at night. How about marketing. There is where I made a number of initial mistakes. After a few years I got it right, and enjoyed it. Lastly, having fun. It took a couple of years until I even took a day off, but like marketing, I found a way to balance things out and have fun both when doing the job and when relaxing outside of the job.

After an almost fifteen year run, we missed living in Phoenix, and decided that for the third time in our life we should move there again. So we sold the property and the business. I am proud to say that I found a great human resources professional, Robert Weaver, who continued to grow the business and maintained the values of serving our clients.

ENTREPRENURIAL BROTHER

I knew two very successful brothers, Ray and Rob. Growing up, they were very energetic workers, doing the usual things to earn some money at a young age. Like many children who seem to always be doing something for income, they did it because they were self-motivated to do so, not because their family was poor and needed the money. Their situation was quite the contrary.

Both fellows were good students, and became college educated. They took part in numerous extra-curricular activities. Avid sportsmen, they each played several sports in high school. Both in high school and college they were popular, and everyone seemed to know them. They were full of life and full of fun.

Ray was almost ten years older than Rob, so entered the workforce earlier. After college, he had several jobs in industrial sales, and did quite well. To be successful in sales, he knew he had to learn the business – everything about it. He observed and learned every aspect he could. This knowledge, plus his engaging ability to build relationships, resulted in making Ray a consistent top salesperson, earning lucrative commissions and bonuses. In his mid-thirties, he decided to go in business for himself. Not just starting out small with a nice little niche of self-employment, Ray had big dreams and was eager to get to them. He wanted to manufacture industrial refrigeration equipment which could compete on a national scale.

Not too many people would have the ability to raise enough money for a start-up business, which needed to build a factory, purchase industrial machinery, and hire a workforce. Several million dollars were needed. But not too many people had the salesmanship skills and business relationships with the right influential people, like Ray. He knew he would not get large loans from banks, so he made deals with many of his contacts to invest in his venture. A number of his clients trusted him and believed in him, and his dream became a reality.

He opened his manufacturing plant and took on the competition. His target market was to go high end – in innovative design features, in service and quality, and in selling price. Bold objectives, but he achieved them.

In the meantime, younger brother Rob graduated from college and went into the Navy. After discharge, his plan was to become a school teacher and a football coach. As he told me, he would have been very happy and content. However, older brother Ray wanted him to work for his company. He convinced him that he would be making many more times the annual income than he ever could teaching school.

He did just that, joined his brother's company. His brother made him start at the bottom to learn the business, but he quickly rose and earned the position of vice president. Both brothers were happy and very wealthy.

This is the stage they were at when I met them. I was a college student at the time. As successful as they were, they both always had time for people. Even just a student like me. Ray was attending a function I was at, and we were introduced. I was extremely impressed when I was invited to visit their facility for a tour of the operations. A few months later I made an appointment and paid the visit. Both Ray and Rob invited me in their offices and told me about their personal histories, and all about the company. I could tell they were both passionate about their business, and enjoyed helping young people.

What I found comical was the difference in their perspectives, as they answered questions and gave career advice. Ray's profound advice was that your goal should always be to own your own business. Work for others to gain experience and learn about the industry, but you can never fulfill your dreams working for somebody else.

Rob's advice was just the opposite – you never want to take the risks of starting your own enterprise. You can go into any field, do a good job, and you will earn an honest living and do very well for yourself. Plus, you will have the peace of mind that you're not risking your own money.

Each was doing very well, were successful businessmen, and did good things for their employees and the community. And each was devoted to, and defined by their work. But they each had a different path through their career, and they were convinced they each did it the best way. In their conversations, they each talked mostly about how smart a person the other brother was. They loved and admired each other, and gave the other person so much credit for the company success. But when giving guidance to younger people, they tried to steer the person to their particular pathway to success.

Chapter 6

Communication

"Let us make a special effort to stop communicating with each other, so we can have some conversation."- Mark Twain

I don't think you can write a book about achieving success without a chapter on communication. While communication might not be the root of all evil, it is definitely the root of all problem solutions. It always seems to be the biggest employee complaint when conducting engagement surveys. Employees always complain there isn't enough communications; management always promises to improve communications.

In today's business world with company intranet, teleconferences and social media, there are so many ways to communicate effectively and keep it entertaining. And the way the media world keeps changing, there are numerous ways to communicate with every employee frequently and timely.

So why does it continue to be such a source of frustration? I think too many people in leadership still look at communication as a top-down message of presenting information to keep people loyal and motivated.

My recommendation is to embrace the whole topic of communication as a skill that should be taught and made a key part of company culture. That is the approach we took several years ago and has produced success. Every employee in the company takes a personal communications assessment and participates in a half-day seminar on communication styles and behavioral patterns. The purpose is to educate everyone on how to improve their communication skills in all facets – interpersonal conversations, emails, presentations, meetings, and achieving team consensus.

If this training results in reducing misunderstandings, avoiding arguments, resolving conflicts, reaching agreements, and improving team collaboration, even to a small extent, it is successful. We have achieved these features to a large extent. The program has indeed become part of the culture, and many people regard it as the most beneficial training they have ever done, both for at home and at work.

There are a variety of consulting and assessment companies available for this type of program. We have utilized the instrument called Connecting With People. There are other similar programs, I'm not promoting any particular brand. What I am encouraging is that every Human Resources leader should do research and implement some type of program for improving communications.

Then set up a plan for everyone. We do executives to interns. Everyone needs this training. Even when people tell us they did it in the past somewhere else, we tell them learning doesn't hurt, it can only do good to go through it again. Why everyone? Well, everyone communicates. In some form or manner, everyone communicates sometimes. And most of us communicate in some form or manner almost all of the time.

Sometimes when I am speaking to groups, I ask if anyone would like to present a short segment of the program. I will show you the material during the next break, and you can present it simply by following the power point. Amazingly, I usually lose all eye contact. With a school audience, I usually get a few hands that want to volunteer. The fact is, so many people have a fear of speaking in front of others. Some studies rate it as the second most common fear next to dying.

Are you kidding me? So I simply ask, how many like to speak, act or perform in front of others, and again, not a whole lot of hands.

Then I ask people to go back in time to when they were in high school, with every opportunity in the world open to them. What would you like to be? Don't worry about the cost of education or other obstacles, if you had a fantasy to become anything you wanted, what would it be? A singer, actor, professional athlete, doctor, lawyer, accountant, detective, politician, CEO, teacher, military leader, small business owner, store manager, stand-up comic, musician, football coach, sportscaster, human resources manager. Hundreds more, the list is endless. But there is not one job which you can do successfully without speaking or performing with other people. I have seen thousands of job descriptions, and have never seen one which states that you can sit alone in a corner and never talk with anyone. If there is, who would have that job as their career goal? You cannot be a successful doctor, lawyer, athlete, actor, singer, teacher, preacher or even bartender, if you cannot speak, act or perform in front of others. So to have career success at anything, you will need to overcome your fear of speaking. And no, the way to do that is not to look at an imaginary line above the audience's heads, or imagining the audience naked, or any of the ridiculous things you may hear. The way to overcome the fear is to learn communications skills. Learn how to convey your thoughts to your audience, and how to modify your style to engage your audience. You are not speaking at your audience, you are conversing with your audience. You will gain confidence in your presentation skills, which will overcome your fear. If you think this sounds too simple, it really is. As Mike Myers stated in the movie Mystery, Alaska, "This is not rocket surgery."

WE NEVER TALK ANYMORE

Unfortunately, teaching communication isn't teaching English. While we as a society have seen social media improve communication capabilities, we have left it kill spelling, grammar, and in some cases even talking.

Families can be observed at a restaurant or even at their home dinner table having a family meal, and every member, even two year olds, are on a mobile device. And no one is talking with each other. The family therapist, which eventually has to be summoned, suggests they have a no-cell zone. Imagine a span of two or three hours, through dinner and a period following, where the family actually looks at each other, has conversations, and shares information about their day. How old is this movie? But after a short time it becomes the norm, and it works wonders.

Now apply this same logic in the workplace – even more difficult. And probably counterproductive because there is too much going on to set time blocks. But you can set meeting rules. Obviously, there are always priority messages and emergency calls. But we can make a rule that during the meetings all phones be put on silent and only absolute emergencies will be responded to. Most can wait until a break. Same with reading and answering emails. Some meetings are of course more informal, but with most scheduled meetings a few simple rules should apply for the meeting to be productive. And definitely out of respect to a speaker or presenter.

We're not going to get too old fashioned here. As business and media jargon, acronyms, meanings to formats, slang, capitalization, full names, whatever, keep changing – teach it. We don't want to resist the way the world is changing, we couldn't. We want to keep everyone up to speed. I don't want to include an example here of a recent change, because by the time you read this, it will be outdated and replaced by something else.

LEARN TO LISTEN

Listening is not the same as hearing. Listening is a skill that can be improved, in probably everyone. Since people communicate with both verbal and non-verbal messages, a listener must focus on the spoken words as well as observe the body language. Communication is usually emotional, so the listener must identify the emotion and acknowledge it. You may have to show empathy or encouragement through your body language to convey your understanding. Sometimes when I'm speaking I think, is a nod or a smile or a grunt really too much to ask.

There are numerous seminars on listening skills. This is another training that everyone should go through. The basic principles are usually somewhat similar. The first is to focus on the speaker. Doesn't matter if you are one on one or attending a conference. Try to clear your mind of other thoughts and focus on the message being presented. Do not be formulating your response or counter opinion before hearing the person through. With some speakers or topics this will be a natural, if they are hitting your passion button. Others may make this task more challenging.

The second principle is to avoid interrupting. Allow the other person to finish their thought and make their point. Some people have a habit of finishing the other person's sentence, or starting a response before the speaker is done, telling their version of the story or something they did that was even better, or worse – changing the subject to another topic and completely ignoring what the speaker was trying to say. These are all terrible listening skills that we must be conscious of.

A third principle is usually about withholding judgement. Being a good listener does not mean you are agreeing with their facts, values, message, or opinion. But it does mean that you withhold your judgement until they have explained theirs. Your body language as a listener will often reveal your disagreement. Again, this should be curtailed until you have the opportunity to respond.

And a fourth principle is usually about showing your interest. Smile, nod, show concern, use verbal acknowledgment that you are understanding, whatever appropriate. This may mean paraphrasing or questioning, like "so you are saying" or "let me be sure if I am following." This is not interrupting, this is active listening.

These are four simple steps to make you a better listener. Hardly a substitute for a listening seminar, but listening is a requirement for being a good communicator. As the Human Resources person, I have often been the deliverer of bad news. I have had hundreds of emotional encounters where I was the one to inform someone they were being disciplined, demoted, laid off, terminated, or even worse – such as informing them of a tragedy or death. These types of messages have to be delivered with grace, compassion, empathy and dignity. You must observe their body language to interpret their state of mind to see if they are understanding. You cannot keep rolling through your delivery if you see that their emotions have totally taken over and they are not hearing anything you are saying. Then you try to have a calm dialog and do more listening.

COMMUNICATION STYLES

Now we will start with the four basic styles of communication. You are going to be all of these at some times, to some degree. You will be predominately one or two of these most of the time. You were most likely born with your primary pattern, and people love you for it. Usually, not always. It defines who you are. It is your thinking pattern. There are times you must recognize that you need to modify your normal style in order to avoid conflict, gather opinions from others, or bring a team to collaboration. You can play your style like a violin, and at other times wear it like a curse. You have to know how to use it, control it, and open your mind to respect others.

There are no good or bad patterns, no pattern that is necessary to do a particular job, and no pattern that is smarter or more productive than any other.

Each style has strengths and benefits they bring to a team. And each style has some drawbacks which can frustrate others, particularly if they do not understand how every person is different in how they think and how they convey what they think.

As in many things, diversity is good. A team will function much better if it has a representative from each of the four primary styles. A well-functioning team, whether they are a work team, a family, or a successful TV show, will show the harmony that happens when everyone knows and adapts to one another's patterns.

You can take a short assessment to discover your own primary and secondary pattern, but for now we will quickly cover the four basic primary patterns. As you are reading, you will probably formulate an opinion of which one you are, and also which one the people closest to you are. Hint, opposites attract, so if you are married you are more likely to have a spouse in a different primary pattern than yourself. Remember what I said about good teams.

DOMINANT PATTERN

People with a Dominant pattern exhibit high-assertive and low-responsive behaviors. They have an outspoken nature, and try to maintain control over their personal feelings. They like to be in charge, and they like to make decisions. It is natural for Dominants to be direct, candid, and possibly forceful in communicating with others. They do not avoid conflict, and prefer to focus on the problem, resolve it, and move on. Dominants control their body movements and expressions, often leaving others with the impression that they are normally serious and abrupt.

Dominants give a high priority to time, and value others who respect their time. Indeed, you may find that many Dominant people are obsessed with time management, always worried about wasting time. They think in the now. What is the best use of our time right now? Thus, if you are attending their meeting, or want their participation, be cautious about wasting too much time on small talk, sports, humor, weather, or anything else other than getting down to business – because we are wasting time.

Dominants like eye contact. When conversing with a Dominant you may wonder why they are always staring at you. They may be wondering why you are not looking at them when you listen and speak. Direct eye contact may be intimidating to some people, but a Dominant interprets it as a sign of trust. They are sometimes close talkers, not only looking the other person in the eye but doing so at close range, often gesturing with a pointing finger.

Dominants also focus on the bottom line. That is their priority; what are the results we want, how are we measuring against them? It goes along with the time element. They will stay on task to achieve the bottom line result. They will participate and gain interest in something if they know what end goal we are seeking. Communications should be direct and to the point, not a lot of words, stories, or flowery language. If you send a long message to a Dominant you better start with bottom line bullet points. If you begin with several paragraphs of prose, your message will likely not get read. In conversation, if you are speaking with too many words and analogy examples, and taking too long to make your point; they will either cut you off or show through their body language that they have grown very impatient.

A Dominant will usually have a serious businesslike attitude, and can become annoyed with those who do not. They are fast-paced and direct, and often speak loud and forceful. Take them seriously, but do not take things personally. A Dominant may seem tough, harsh and opinionated to others; but they are just serious and focused, and their direct and loud response is their usual manner, not meant to be insulting. You can see why there are often misunderstandings here. As a Human Resources person, I am often asked to resolve conflicts between people. Often the problem is simply the misunderstanding of different communication styles, which after a while leads to two people not wanting to work together because of personality differences. Fortunately, these situations are usually repairable.

Finally, if you are a Dominant, be careful about direct eye contact and personal space. When getting intense, try to calm down, back off some space, slow down the pace, lower the tone, and even smile. Not everything is on fire. Also, ask more – tell less. Dominants often phrase things in a telling fashion. "Bring an agenda for everyone and an extra tablet." Spoken like it's a direct order. Even when giving directions. "You're going to go south for three blocks, then you're going to make a right turn."

And please try to be less protective of your time. You may have a child who constantly wants to play with you. "Daddy, sit on the floor with me and we'll play this game." How do you respond? "OK, I'm reading something right now, you start and tell me when it's my turn." All they really want is some of your time. It's easy to see with a children's example; but the same type of thing may be happening with others in your life – family, employees, coworkers – and you are not seeing it.

Another common example is with something as simple as shopping at the mall with the family. After the desired purchases are made, it's time to head for home. Walking past a new store, someone might suggest we go in and check this out. The immediate reaction of the Dominant may be something like "I thought we were leaving." Then on the way home, someone suggests we venture out of the way a few blocks to see if the new restaurant being built is open yet. The Dominant's reaction, "How long is that going to take?" Even though there is nothing else on the schedule, nothing waiting at home to do, it is still thought of as wasting time. If you are a Dominant, your obsession with time may be controlling you.

Dominants are great to have on a team because they help to keep the group focused and on schedule. They make decisions, and will take charge if needed. They can see chaos and get everyone back on track. However, if misunderstood, they can be perceived as pushy, bossy (even if it's not their job), unemotional, uncaring, sarcastic. Only about 12% of the population are Dominant, so they must learn how to better modify their pattern and pace, and mellow out sometimes. People who are not Dominant need to recognize they are just intense, and try to adapt to their time priorities and direct style.

So are you a Dominant? Do you work for a Dominant? Are you married to a Dominant? Do you have a coworker, child, friend or customer who is a Dominant? Probably there are several of these questions that got a yes answer. Like all styles, there are Dominant personalities in most parts of your work and social life. Understanding them and how they typically react and respond, will make interactions more productive and enjoyable.

EXPRESSIVE PATTERN

People with an Expressive pattern naturally exhibit high-assertive and high-responsive behaviors. They communicate easily and comfortably, and are more open in their gestures and expressions than the other patterns. Expressives are very people oriented. They desire a clear and open show of understanding by both sides in communication, and they use persuasion and exaggerated body movements to promote that understanding. Expressives are recognized as being energetic, emotional, opinionated, sometimes loud, and always ready to take risks and volunteer. They are also playful and fun loving, tend to dislike routine, and may at times appear to be unfocused in their work.

Expressives place a high value on relationships. They are naturally skilled and comfortable at establishing and maintaining interpersonal relationships. They prefer to take the time and get to know each other before moving right into a serious business discussion. Quite different than a Dominant in this aspect. See why it's important for two people to understand each other's styles to improve communications. Here is one small example where one could frustrate the other or prevent a strong relationship from forming, just because they have different social styles.

Expressives like to have fun. Of course everyone likes to have fun, but to an Expressive, it's a priority. Fun first, then we'll get the work done. Why would anyone want to do any job if it wasn't fun? And their idea of fun is contagious. They make sure everyone is having a good time. They are good story tellers, natural entertainers. They will make a project fun for the whole team.

Along with fun and relationships, Expressives are animated, full of high energy, a lot of movement, gestures, and facial expressions. Their voice fluctuates in pitch and volume as they get excited. They do a lot of smiling and touching.

Expressives have a hard time saying no, and as a result will often over commit themselves or their team to an almost impossible deadline. Others may perceive this as insincere or phony in their promises; but it is because they try to please everyone and will put burden on themselves to strengthen the relationship. They can also talk fast and quickly change topics, thinking as they are speaking. Thus, sometimes what they say is not what they mean – they were literally "just thinking out loud."

Where Dominants were bottom line focused, Expressives are big picture focused. If you need their engagement, start with the big picture. Expressives become quickly bored with details and over analysis. They always think big picture and future. They are good visionaries and forecasters. Naturally creative, they will usually come up with more features, ideas and options. And they can get others on board. They have a talent for inspiring and persuading others, because they have such natural excitement and effective use of words to make their point. But they are impulse buyers, and can quickly run with new ideas, only to think it through later and change their mind.

About 19% of people are Expressive, and you may feel like you've met them all. Their high energy and fun-first attitude can at times be draining on others, particularly when you are in a serious mode. Amazingly, they can be as productive as any other pattern. They just seem to work at a different pace. They can work fast, then stop, bother everyone else, then go back and work fast again.

I am an Expressive, so is my wife. Yes, we are one of a very small percentage of married couples where both have the same primary pattern. How dangerous are two Expressives without the check and balance of the other three? It might explain why we have just built a new home – our 18th address. We like to buy a house, remodel it, then sell it and move to another house. It's always an adventure. Remember I said Expressives are impulse buyers, they are with big purchases too. Research, comparison shopping, ratings, consumer reports – boring. Did I mention Expressives like change?

Expressives are great to have on a team because they keep it light and fun. They make sure we don't take ourselves too seriously. They are also the ones to keep the vision in mind, are the big picture thinkers. Expressives also operate at a contagious high energy. Just remember to paraphrase and playback agreements and understandings, so they remember their commitments. Confirm information and timelines.

Are you an Expressive? Do you work for an Expressive? Are you married to an Expressive? Do you have a coworker, child, friend or customer who is an Expressive? There are surely Expressive personalities in most parts of your work and social life. Life would certainly be less fun without them.

ANALYTICAL PATTERN

Analytical patterns are by nature less assertive and less responsive in their behaviors than the other patterns. This means they are reserved in the way they express themselves and they are controlled in their outward gestures and actions.

Analyticals are task oriented, and are very careful to be certain to get the job done right the first time. They focus on facts and details, examine all options, rely on past experience, and tend to be systematic and cautious in making decisions. Analyticals also tend to be disciplined with the use of time and are thorough in their work. They may prefer to work alone, appear detached from emotions, and might seem more concerned with information than with people.

An Analytical person likes to have fun, but definitely puts their priority in order of work first, fun second. They are in a serious mode more often than not, particularly when concentrating on a task.

Very process oriented, they are good at developing a system, be it a procedure, schedule, outline, agenda, charts, graphs or checklist. Then they will maintain and measure steps and progress accordingly. They like to have a detailed plan before getting started.

Analyticals are thinkers, and take their time to think before responding. When asked a question, they will not only think their response through, but they are generating more questions with detail that perhaps was left vague – what timeframe are you needing, in what context do you want the answer, do you want all transactions or just current ones, etc., etc. As a result, a question or request for their opinion may be met with a blank stare and silence for several seconds, while they are thinking their response through. Often their response then includes several more questions for clarity. Now, to a Dominant or Expressive, not known for their patience, these several seconds of no response may seem like an eternity. Again, it is a matter of understanding one another's thinking and speaking patterns.

Most, but not all, Analyticals are meticulous and orderly. Even the ones who are not, seem to know where everything is. If you want to drive an Analytical nuts, just mess with their stuff! Pick up something from their desk and look at it, then put it back in the wrong place. They will be stressed until you leave so they can move it back to its proper place. They usually have a system for everything. I once asked an Analytical if he still has the product booklet that came with every tool and appliance he ever purchased. He responded with great pride that he not only has them, but each one is placed in a plastic protective sleeve and filed according to category – kitchen, housewares, garden, shop tools, automotive, and such.

Likewise, an Analytical would never venture to the supermarket without a list. Prior to leaving the house the list is usually rewritten by store section – frozen foods, cleaning supplies, meats, dairy, and such, again bringing more detail and efficiency to the plan. They don't do too much without a list. A list helps them to plan ahead, and they are always more comfortable when they plan ahead. Take an agenda. To an Analytical, a meeting without an agenda is a recipe for chaos. They want an agenda for every meeting, preferably ahead of time so they can come thoroughly prepared.

Does the Analytical pattern sound like you? 32% of people are in the Analytical category. So you are probably close to someone who matches this description. If you are an Analytical, remember to tell people when you need time to think. And let them know that you may need specific information and understanding before getting started.

Analyticals are great to have on the team because they will make sure there is order, sanity, and a process in place. They will think of things that others will not take the time to. And while others may be over committing and charging ahead with their excitement, the Analytical will hold everyone

back and make sure we have a plan and resources before we start off on the wrong foot. How often have we had a chaotic situation, then remember the Analytical in the group who tried to warn us?

AMIABLE PATTERN

People with an Amiable pattern are naturally low assertive and high responsive in their behaviors, meaning they are not forceful in their communication, but they do outwardly show concern and understanding for others. Amiables are the most common classification, with 37% of the population showing this pattern. Amiables are people oriented and team oriented. They are concerned with the happiness and satisfaction of all.

Peacemakers by nature, they are diplomatic, cooperative, patient, and strive to avoid conflict. Generally slower paced and softer spoken than the other patterns. Amiables are tentative and cautious in decision making, less apt to take risks than other styles, and may at times appear non-committal and conforming.

Amiables are foremost about the team or the group. They are genuinely support players, and will do whatever is best for the group. As a result they are very adept at gathering consensus. They are great compromisers.

They are also the best listeners of all patterns. While most people are thinking of their response, Amiables are sincerely listening. Likewise, they are usually polite and non-offensive in their dialog. They will ask for a favor, not tell someone what to do.

Being such good team players, they like to work within their set parameters and permission. They want to know the rules and boundaries so they do not violate them. This is another trait driven by their high priority to avoid conflict. They are perfectionists, and relatively quiet by nature – not prone to speak up in groups. They cherish their personal space. Consistent and loyal workers, they are motivated by both relationships and tasks, and will stick to a job and get it done.

Unfortunately, Amiables are generally the worst procrastinators. They don't like to be rushed. Based on their fear of making a mistake and propensity to meander off topic, they have a tendency to put things off until the last minute. If you are leading a group, you may have to make a real effort to get the Amiable members to speak up and contribute. They may have a great idea or comment, but will be more hesitant to share it in front of others. When forced to make a decision, they would prefer hearing from everyone else first. Even in a simple restaurant setting, the Amiable will usually ask others what they are ordering, then tell the wait staff to "get the others people first then come back to me." They can have a difficult time making even a simple decision, then second guess themselves afterwards.

Might you be an Amiable? If not, you definitely know a few. Remember to give them time and space, and know that they function best in a calm atmosphere.

TEAM IMPLICATIONS

As stated previously, a team will function best when there is a diverse blend of patterns. Of course, that does not always exist. So we will explore the team dynamics that exist through all patterns, then realize what may be missing when there is no member of a particular pattern.

Purpose and direction. What is the purpose of our team? If we cannot answer that, do we have any chance of success? Well, various patterns view this matter differently. A Dominant may view the whole purpose and direction of the team is about outcomes. Bottom line. Results. Why else would we be here?

An Expressive may view the purpose and direction of the team as possibilities. Big picture. Vision. This project can lead to future engagements and successful growth.

While an Analytical may define our purpose and direction as methods. What methods and systems will be utilized? What controls? Operations manuals, policies and procedures.

The Amiable is thinking impact. What is the impact on the company, the team, the customer, our business partners?

Roles and responsibilities. Each member of the team knows they have roles and responsibilities, but their natural pattern will make them view these things differently. A Dominant will feel their role is to delegate. Sometimes regardless of their position, they have a natural instinct to take charge and will delegate assignments to others. Have you ever experienced this? Pretty easy to see how this can cause problems.

Whereas an Expressive will see their role to volunteer. They may volunteer themselves or volunteer the whole team. "Sure, we'd be happy to do it." After all, that's why we are here.

An Analytical believes their role is to question. Play Devil's advocate. Challenge the process.

An Amiable will see their role as one of cooperation. We're here for the good of the team, how can we do our part? We can bring consensus to the group.

Team meetings. Something as simple as scheduled team meetings should not be difficult to run efficiently. But is the reason for even having them felt the same by all? Actually no. Dominants view a meeting purpose as one to report and measure progress. Again, it's all about the bottom line.

An Expressive wants team meetings for the purpose of sharing. I want everyone else to know what I'm doing; and I want to know what everyone else is working on. That way we will appreciate one another's efforts.

An Analytical views the meeting to again ensure that we are following the plan. We're on the right step of the process, on schedule, measurements in place.

An Amiable comes to the meeting to support. Who needs help? Is everyone caught up, can we make things easier on anyone?

Team Decision Making. How do we make team decisions and what do we base them on? Can we function effectively as a team if we are not viewing decision making through the same lens? Well, a Dominant will base a decision on the risk and reward. They make decisions with their gut based on whatever information they have available.

An Expressive makes decisions more emotional based with the focus on future impact. Where will this get us down the road? Long-term thinking over short-term thinking.

The Analytical is the historian, and will base decisions on past actions. What worked for us in the past? What have we tried before that didn't work, we don't want to repeat past mistakes. As a rule, Expressives are thinking in the future, Analyticals are thinking in the past, and Dominants are thinking in the now.

As for Amiables, they are more concerned with maintaining the status quo. Let's not rock the boat. Base decisions on harmony and a steady course.

Motivation and engagement. Like the other elements, the dynamics of a team are interpreted differently from people with different patterns. The things that will motivate a Dominant are input and control. Fulfilling their need to provide input, and their desire to control. The team environment may or may not always be conducive to meeting these needs.

An Expressive will be motivated by their opportunity to show their enthusiasm, and aggressively getting involved. Simply put, if they can see fun and passion in the project they will be a dynamite team member. If they are bored, not so much.

The Analytical will find motivation in the openness to discuss the process and avoid mistakes. Helping to keep the team on the most efficient and effective course of action while striving to get it right the first time.

And the Amiable will find motivation in being able to quietly participate for the good of the team, seeing everyone gain recognition for the group effort. They are engaged by the spirit of cooperation.

Communication is a wonderful thing, but an inexact science that must always be worked on. I'm convinced that through conscious effort and training, everyone's interpersonal skills can be improved. I also think this is the single most overlooked area for training and analysis in today's business world. Many organizations train in presentation skills, but to make profound change and understanding, we must get down to the individual thinking and communication patterns.

Chapter 7

The Beloved Boss – Realistic
or Oxymoron?

"In the past a leader was a boss. Today's leaders must be partners with their people, they no longer can lead solely based on positional power."- Ken Blanchard

I never liked the word boss, as either a verb or a noun. There have been many times in social settings, where someone introduced me to a friend or family member, and they said "he's my boss." I would always comment "we work together, I'm nobody's boss." I find the term boss to be embarrassing, and I don't like the implication. It may stem from the old prison gang movies, where the mean and evil prison guards were always addressed as "boss." It has a connotation of fear and subservience.

Of course the term is widely used and understood, and I'm not going to change that. I think we've all experienced good bosses and bad bosses, maybe in the same person. We can learn a lot from both types.

THE BAD BOSS

Let's start with bad bosses. We've all seen too many of them. Often egomaniacs who take all the credit for the good, none of the blame for the bad. They drive employees to work longer and faster, while holding no such standards for themselves. I find it almost comical that Urban Dictionary lists Simon Legree as a noun meaning a cruel employer who demands excessive work from the employees. Simon Legree was of course the evil slave owner in the novel Uncle Tom's Cabin written by Harriet Beecher Stowe. A book published in 1852 that helped lay the groundwork for the civil war, based largely from the anti-slavery anger stirred up by the Simon Legree character. So if you are a boss and called a Simon Legree, you must be a much disliked manager.

The main objection I have against these bad bosses isn't as much their actions as their attitude. They have a genuinely inflated opinion of themselves and a sense of entitlement that they really deserve to have power over others. They will not participate in training and development programs because they feel they know it all, what more could anyone teach them? You may engage them in discussion, but they have already dismissed most opinions that disagree with theirs. People often come to me to talk about the difficulty of working with such a boss, and question all company leadership for placing and supporting this type of person in a management role.

There are many types of bad bosses. They may be sexist, racist, screamers, micro managers, play favorites, tell lies, unqualified, don't care that you have an outside life. If you have one, is there anything you can do other than quitting your job? Well yes, hopefully it doesn't come to that.

First, be honest with yourself. Is the boss really that bad, consistently? And how are you really doing? Are you performing good work, are you maintaining your knowledge, are you showing a positive attitude? You will lose the sympathy vote if you are displaying a negative attitude or spreading negative gossip.

Approach the situation like a project. Compile a list of the actions or behaviors that you found troubling. List some options that would have been better, or comments that should have been said that would have explained the situation and perhaps avoided the bad feelings. Then request a meeting and share your thoughts with your boss. Tell him or her that your intentions are to improve the relationship and work environment. They likely are not fully aware of how they are perceived. Maybe they are and don't care, but hopefully they will respect your concern and professionalism in your desire to improve the situation. You may be doing many coworkers a favor, as well as your boss. Of course, this could be a big risk, depending on the attitude of the boss and their openness for criticism. Be prepared to get a backlash that their behavior may be based on your performance, attendance, attitude, whatever. That is probably the case to some degree, and as adults you can clear the air and both vow to improve the relationship and support each other.

If the situation is too far gone, too serious, maybe based on an improper relationship or ethics violation, or if you tried the above and it made the relationship worse, or if there is any type of retaliation; it is time to get help. The first place to turn, and the safest, is Human Resources.

Everyone probably has their worst boss in mind. I have worked with several and have seen many. My personal worst rises to the top. Believe me, I have experienced the worst of bad bosses. If there was a national convention of bad bosses, mine would win the award for "The Number 1 Baddest Boss." I will call him Charles. I wasn't with this company too long, because of Charles. Frankly, I don't think he had a single friend within the company. Everybody talked about him, even people outside of his function. Like myself, a number of people had left the company because of Charles. This was a big company and he had a big job. How he got to this level was what everyone found unbelievable. He actually didn't last too long. About a year after I left I heard he was fired. His tenure with this particular company was about four or five years, but he left a lot of collateral damage. I can't imagine him being successful elsewhere, but hopefully he did find a better match. What made Charles so bad? He exhibited many of the negative elements of a bad boss – yelling and screaming, blaming others for anything that went bad, giving no one else credit, and such. However, the main ingredient in his failure was his own insecurity. Charles was paranoid, possibly because he knew he was underqualified for his role in basic technical knowledge. But more than that, he did not have the interpersonal skills or engaging personality that are requirements for success in any leadership position. When people have that self-realization, they know they cannot inspire people through positive relationships, so their alternative is to lead by fear. Constantly threatening and demeaning people, trying to lead solely on position power, fortunately will not last long.

Many good people have been lost because of bad bosses. As stated earlier, people don't quit a job, they quit their boss. If the situation is so unbearable that it is affecting your happiness, at work and at home, something must be done. That may mean trying to transfer internally or looking for a new job elsewhere. Sometimes that is simply the easiest solution, and may turn out to be the best decision you ever made. But if you love the company and really don't want to leave, try to improve the relationship. Bad bosses can become good bosses. I have spent a great deal of my career helping people with this transformation. Are you the bad boss who would like to change? Every supervisor can improve their skills. All it takes is self-awareness and the desire to change.

In the great book by Marshall Goldsmith, What Got You Here Won't Get You There, he talks about qualities that leaders must have to become successful. Two of them are Apologizing and Thanking. In fact, each of these has its own chapter in the book. I don't see what is hard about sincerely apologizing to another person when you made an error in judgement, or falsely accused someone. Nor do I understand how it could be difficult to say "thank you" to someone who did you a favor.

Yet there are people in leadership positions who make apologizing or thanking an extremely rare occurrence. You may find this hard to believe, but it is why Marshall Goldsmith gave these attributes two chapters in his book. There are some leaders who feel they are so powerful that they would find it embarrassing to ever apologize for a mistake. In fact, they would never even admit to a mistake. Thanking is another skill they have not developed. That would mean someone else could share credit for something under their control.

These people clearly fall into the bad bosses category. We may never understand how they got their job, or how they keep their job; but in a way I feel sorry for them – they are not happy people. They are in love with their power, but are not personally fulfilled, and everyone around them is miserable.

THE GOOD BOSS

Hopefully everyone has had experiences with good bosses. Someone who you would follow into a war. Someone with whom you share mutual trust and respect. Someone who you feel has a genuine concern for your career and happiness.

A good boss is a good listener, always finding time to listen to people's ideas, suggestions, questions and concerns. A good boss is open and truthful. There are always things which must remain confidential for the time, but they will explain that – not display an arrogant attitude that they know something you don't. "I'm in the executive circle – you don't have a need to know." A good boss would never think like that.

A good boss sets a good example by taking on difficult tasks and working tirelessly, never expecting their people to work longer and harder than they do. They also make sure their people have all the information, tools and resources to do their job. They don't leave people set up to fail. They recognize when people need help, training or support, and see to it that it is furnished.

They also get to know their people as unique individuals, and respect and treat them accordingly. Sometimes managers have said to me things like "I am a strict rater, I never give a rating above a 4." Some go the opposite way, "I am lenient with everybody, and I would never give a low appraisal because I want to give encouragement." I always suggest to them that they should strive to be a fair rater, and give people the truth they deserve. It's not about you, an honest rating should be something all employees deserve. As a manager, you can never say you will always handle a given situation the same. Every situation is unique, circumstances may be different, communications may be different, and people are definitely different. A good boss must always be open minded, flexible and fair.

A good boss is a good communicator and gives clear expectations and feedback. This is all part of coaching, which is something that many managers do not realize is a requirement of their job. Too often when someone is made a first time supervisor, they are told "congratulations, you are now a supervisor" without much further instruction. They know their responsibilities now include scheduling people, taking attendance, making sure there is coverage, preparing sales and customer reports, and keeping the place clean and orderly. What is often overlooked is to convey that their duties now include teaching, inspiring and motivating people. These are some complex skills that have to be learned. A good boss will inform you of this role, and make sure you become equipped to handle it. This is a long term commitment. The good boss will have the compassion, patience and understanding so you do not fail.

I have been blessed to have worked with many great bosses. In the book dedication section I mentioned Jim Swanson, who invites and encourages open discussion and appreciates differing opinions. Another admirable leader I worked with was Joe Fassler. Joe was also a leader who sincerely appreciated a challenging viewpoint. Even after he announced a decision, he would be open to hearing that it was not working, and should possibly be rescinded or changed. These two CEO's had a strong compassion for people, always gave recognition to their people, always tried to be fair, and above all had a great sense of humor. They knew when not to take themselves too seriously, and they could turn a room filled with tension into a lighthearted moment with their warm smile and timely remarks. That is a natural talent all leaders should have, but many do not. I have seen these men maintain their composure many times through situations that could have exploded into heated arguments.

Another wonderful person I reported to was Ardon Schambers. Ardon had a gift for bringing a team together, and making everyone feel they had a special expertise to share. He had great collaboration skills, and his team had a special bond. But Ardon's most memorable characteristic was that he made sure everyone was having fun. I cannot remember a day when we didn't laugh.

The boss who was my greatest mentor was in my first job out of college. I reported to a terrific leader, Betty Underkoffler. Betty was a strong manager and forceful decision maker, but very fair and compassionate. I worked for Betty for about five years, and learned more from her than from anyone since. A definite role model and influence on my own management career.

Good bosses make successful companies. The good news is that great leaders are made, not born. Some of the best managers are those who acknowledge that they may not be the smartest person on a particular topic, but they will listen, keep an open mind, and never stop learning.

LEADERSHIP STYLES

Becoming a beloved boss can be a learned experience. That doesn't mean it is easy, changing behavior is always a difficult challenge. And there are two elements – behavior and style. Most of us have had role models, and like many things in life, we are the products of our environment. We tend to emulate the management style of the people who managed us. This may not be in our best interest. The study of management is an ongoing science, and the models we grew up with may be outdated in today's more sophisticated age of technology, information, and changing work values.

I read an article which explained the nuances of twenty different management styles. Obviously, trying to split hairs between that many defined styles makes for a lot of blending. Better to look at a few key styles and determine which one is most effective in today's business world. People were born with their primary communication style, whereas leadership styles are developed.

Autocratic Leadership: Let's take the three main categories of management styles, and like communication styles, we can move from one to another as circumstances dictate. The first common style is autocratic leadership. Old fashioned, power driven, and high control. Its success is based on obedience to authority. The boss sees himself as a dictator, and treats employees as workers whose job is to do as they're told. Obviously, this is not the component of a beloved boss, and has diminishing effectiveness with the modern workforce.

Paternalistic Leadership: The second category is that of a paternalistic leader. This kind of leadership is one in which the leader views themselves like a parent to those led. They may be very protective of employees and overly concerned with their potential failure. Many managers and businesses are proud to use this method, feeling they take care of their people, although they do put the needs of the organization first. However, this approach operates more on compliance rather than real individual motivation.

Servant Leadership: The third category encompasses several related styles, such as participative, coaching, visionary and servant leadership. Participative in that it represents a medium between over controlling and laissez faire styles. The manager gets involved with the people and participates, not dictates. The leader provides a good ethical example and gains respect. This type of successful leader is also a coach who possesses the ability to teach and train. They groom people to improve both their knowledge and skill. They also communicate the vision and make sure everyone understands the big picture and expected outcomes. Lastly, the leader shares a servant style in which he or she operates socially and has a priority to benefit the workers. This approach emphasizes certain positive values such as trust, honesty and fairness. They treat people as partners. This is clearly the mark of a healthy organization, and will earn the title of beloved boss.

The servant leadership approach goes beyond employee-related behavior and calls for a rethinking of the hierarchical relationship between leaders and subordinates. This does not mean that the ideal of a participative style in any situation is diminished, but that the focus of leadership responsibilities is the promotion of performance and satisfaction of employees.

The highest priority of a servant leader is to encourage, support and enable subordinates to unfold their full potential and abilities. This leads to an obligation to delegate responsibility and engage in participative decision-making.

THE LITTLE GUY / THE BIG GUY

I think most people know a role of Human Resources is to be the spokesperson for employees. It is a role we accept and take very seriously. Sometimes the employee has no other representation, and they feel Human Resources is the only place they can trust to explain their situation. It's the Little Guy against the big, bad giants of industry. So HR often is in the position of standing up for the Little Guy. After becoming aware of a problem, we commence an impartial investigation for facts and conduct many interviews; in order to find the truth, make corrective actions to improve the situation, and recommend fair and proper treatment for all parties involved. This is what we do quite frequently. Sometimes the employee's concerns are well justified; sometimes they are definitely not.

A role that occurs more rarely is when we sometimes have to stand up for the Big Guy. The people in charge, which could be the CEO, the head coach, the school principal – are often alone at the top. Information is frequently hidden or filtered before it reaches them. And they are often the person blamed for everything that goes wrong. Like with employees, sometimes the shots directed at senior leadership are unjustified; while other times the leaders can be their own worst enemy.

It is the duty of HR, or any other trusted "wingmen" to maintain an open relationship with their respective leaders, and give them honest counseling and advice. We want all employees to be successful, and we need our leaders to be successful. They in turn need our help and support, and they may be very reluctant to ask for it. Few people tell a leader when they have made a good decision, or communicated something very effectively. Likewise, even fewer will inform them they handled a situation poorly, made an unwise decision, or used an unprofessional method of communication.

We can help employees improve, we can improve ourselves, and we can help our leaders become the beloved boss we all desire.

The Team Leader
- Darren Thompson

What does it mean to be a leader?
It takes more than being a reader.
You got to be able to take control,
Inspire everyone to reach their goal.

A leader isn't always the boss,
They stay calm amongst chaos,
Can be strong but also care,
Keeps their head and hardly swears.

Part of the team making it whole,
You at the center, the heart and the sole.
Decisions to make, some hard choices,
When something goes wrong you are their voices.

It's never easy, but what is?
As I found out writing this.
You ask me again what does it take.
Just be yourself, for goodness sake.

Chapter 8

Achieving Personal Success

"People who believe they can succeed see opportunities where others see threats."- Marshall Goldsmith

The three "A's" – Approval, Acceptance and Appreciation. That's what we all want. But is that the definition of success? Actually, yes, it should be. Success is satisfaction, and if we achieve those three A's, we should feel satisfaction. Some people have more complex requirements for feeling success, such as winning – being declared the victor. However, as Ben Zander states, "Whenever you have a winner and loser situation, that is a downward spiral conversation." You shouldn't always have to defeat someone else as a requirement for success. In a sports contest yes, but not in business or in life.

To some people, success is measured in wealth or title. This is a very shallow and selfish way to gauge success. Success is the feeling of happiness and fulfillment, and many proud people have found this in all walks of life. Conversely, many people with more wealth and power than most of us can ever imagine, lead unhappy, lonely and empty lives.

So much is written about success and how to achieve it. First we have to make it personal and define what it means to us. We cannot chase success by other people's standards. It seems we often envy people who are successful by our judgement, but they are not satisfied. They appear to have everything, but they don't seem happy.

Look at the priorities in your life. In what areas do you seek approval, acceptance and appreciation? Hopefully there are many. That will be your goal – to attain approval, acceptance and appreciation in the areas that are important to you. This will likely include your career, your role as a spouse and parent, a neighbor, a coach, scout leader, church committee member, and numerous more. And when will you know you have found success in any of those facets – when you feel satisfaction, happiness and fulfillment. It's great to be recognized, and many people are given awards large and small. That is public recognition of approval, acceptance and appreciation. Confirms it! But a lot of your satisfaction, happiness and fulfillment may not result in an award. Indeed, you may gain those feelings by helping someone else get the award and recognition, and you couldn't be happier. That's why success is personal, and it is your standard to measure up to, and yours alone.

What is your purpose? Why did you choose the career you are in? What do you want to accomplish? You have to start with asking yourself questions like these. We cannot charge ahead to accomplish something if we don't know what we are looking for. This may take some deep thinking and self-questioning to determine if you are indeed in the right role. And if you determine you are not, then make a change. It's never too late.

Next, get serious and formal about your chosen path. Write your personal mission statement. As you go through life you can always make changes, but just like a company mission statement, this should be your reminder and your guide of what you want to accomplish and how you want to do it. I will share mine, something I prepared several years ago and have framed in my office. I read it periodically to remind myself of my goal and purpose. I find it to be a good motivational tool, and helps me to stay focused.

Mission Statement
Laman C G Snyder

To serve an organization and its people as a dynamic Leader of the Human Resources function, and drive the people side of the business to accomplish operational objectives. I will establish an environment to encourage open communications, continuous professional development, best management practices, legislative and ethical workplace compliance; plus inspire people to realize their potential, contribute through involvement and participation, feel sincere pride in the organization, strive to achieve excellence, and absolutely enjoy their job.

Admittedly it would be too long for an organization's mission statement. I have wrestled with removing some of the lines, but felt that I needed to cover the various thoughts, so it works for me. When you are doing your own personal mission statement, there are no rules. If you do not have one, I encourage you to give it a shot and you will see how it provides direction and purpose.

The next thing you need after you have a personal mission statement is to identify your own personal Board of Directors. You need trusted advisors who will have a sincere desire in helping you succeed, and are wise enough to help guide you, with both encouragement and caution, as the need arises. I often put people through the following exercise: Draw an oval on a piece of paper and put your name at one end. That is your board table. Now, around the table write in your personal board of directors. The people you go to for advice, the people you share new ideas with, the people who encourage you to proceed, and the people who hold you back when you haven't thought through the downside. How many people are on your board? Does it include your boss? It probably includes your spouse and some other relatives – but not all of your relatives! There are some you would likely never want on your board. Anyway, this is your inner circle. You probably share a lot of trust and respect with the named individuals. It's very informal, and they do not know they are on your board. But it's an honor and a compliment, so you should tell them. Let them know how much you respect and appreciate their opinion and advice. It will strengthen the relationship, and set a venue for expectations that you will advise one another in difficult decisions.

A word of caution, do not go exclusively with your inner circle. To grow and broaden your perspective, you have to reach beyond your established inner circle of trusted friends. After a time the inner circle may become predictable and change adverse. It is your safety net. Therefore, seeking new perspectives will open new pathways and broaden your horizons.

Another word of caution, keep your expectations in check. While everything being said is to generate optimism toward achieving your dreams, and setting a course of action to put your plan in place, you do not want to spend your life chasing unattainable goals. This was a big realization for me to overcome. Always an optimist, I too often thought I could bring every problem to a successful win-win outcome. However, we simply can't fix every problem, improve every person, or cure every illness. We may gain a lot of satisfaction in trying, and that may be our success right there – we addressed the problem and did something about it. Celebrate your small successes, and don't be afraid to reach for the stars. Just don't look at anything short of complete goal attainment as a failure.

VARIOUS PERSPECTIVES ON PERSONAL SUCCESS

"To succeed in life you need two things: Ignorance and Confidence." - Mark Twain

There is a lot of truth in that quote. You need ignorance from all of the negativity that will tell you that you can't do it. What Ben Zander refers to as the voices in the head. If you allow all the imaginary barriers to take control, you will never try. If your idea seems too radical for some, you're too old to change, you will sacrifice too much, and all of the other arguments you will hear, you may need ignorance to their opinions and go with your heart. Here is where your inner circle may be too conservative. The second element is confidence. Once you make a commitment, you need to have the confidence that you will succeed. I have seen a lot of success based on enthusiasm alone. Enthusiasm breeds confidence.

"If I would have listened to what other people told me they needed, I would have spent my entire life developing faster horses." - Henry Ford

Here Henry Ford is telling us to go with our own instincts, our own vision. Sometimes there is comfort and security in following the common thinking. But if you want to really make an impact, don't be afraid to get creative. Think outside the box. Sometimes the greater the risk, the greater the satisfaction.

"Success consists of going from failure to failure without loss of enthusiasm."- Winston Churchill

Persistence and perseverance are key ingredients to success. Very few successes are scored on the first attempt. Failures and setbacks only serve to make the eventual success more rewarding. Again, your confidence and enthusiasm will carry you to the successful outcome.

"80% of success in life can be achieved by just showing up."- Woody Allen

When success involves competition, this can be especially true. From job interviews, to product presentations, to sporting events, time and again your competition either doesn't show up at all, or shows up totally unprepared. The point is, don't rule yourself out. It's not the person who is the most qualified who gets the job, it is the person who performs the best interview. So when you get an opportunity, prepare yourself, have confidence, give it your best shot, and enjoy it.

There are four required elements to achieving personal success. They are potential, attitude, energy and values. To achieve success; to earn approval, acceptance and appreciation; to feel satisfaction, happiness and fulfillment; you need all four. In most things you attempt, a combination of any three of these elements will come up short. Each is a necessary piece of the formula.

Chapter 9

Potential

"There was never a winner who wasn't first a beginner." - Dennis Waitley

The first ingredient for success is potential. You need to have it. You can't be everything. I realized early on that I was not going to make it in this life as a singer. I also accepted the fact that I would never play in the National Basketball Association. I just didn't have the tools. That's ok. Because if we just rule out the very few things we likely are not equipped for, we will find everything else in the world is a possibility. Some things will come more easily than others, but we do possess the potential to become most anything we desire. Remember the Army recruiting slogan, "Be All You Can Be." Well, you can be a lot. You have the potential to learn, develop skills and knowledge, to qualify for most any opportunity.

I often ask an audience how many people can speak three or more languages fluently. Sometimes a hand or two goes up. I admire people who can speak more than one language. Next I ask how many can play at least three different musical instruments. Again, sometimes a hand or two goes up. But usually no hands go up. Then I ask how many can run a marathon. This usually gets some response, but not too many. Then I remind the audience that we are speaking about potential, so every hand should have gone up for every question.

All of us can speak three or more languages, we have the ability to learn. We just have not had the desire or dedicated the time and effort to learn the language skills. But we could. Same for musical instruments. We could learn to play several different instruments, we just have not chosen to take the lessons and practice in order to become accomplished at different instruments. But we could.

How about running a marathon. Same response. Most of us have not had the desire to make the commitment to train and condition ourselves mentally and physically to run a marathon. But we could. In all three of these challenges, we have the potential to do it. Whether we utilize that potential is another matter.

So the most difficult decision is often, what do we want to become? What talents and skills do we want to develop? Where is our true interest and passion? Sadly, many people wander their whole life in search of these answers, and are never really sure if they found their true destiny. We all have so much undeveloped potential.

"The poorest guy in the human race, can have a million-dollar face."
- Burma Shave

This comical Burma Shave sign from 1953 sums it up. He may be the poorest guy in the world, but he can have a million-dollar face. Of course, assuming he uses Burma Shave. The analogy is that the potential of being a million dollar model is right there, undiscovered, while he toils unsuccessfully to make a living.

It is not so much discovering our potential as it is to discover what we want to do, then utilizing our potential to reach that goal. In almost all cases, the potential is there. And we're not going to be great right away. Nobody is. As the quote by Dennis Waitley states, "There was never a winner who wasn't first a beginner." Skills and talent must be groomed, developed and practiced. Michael Jordan didn't make the varsity basketball team his sophomore year in high school. He spent that year again on the junior varsity team. In the great book Outliers by

Malcolm Gladwell, he relates stories of highly successful people, from Bill Gates to The Beatles, and gives the threshold of 10,000 hours of practice to truly master your abilities at such a high level.

How hard is it to find your potential, or to decide on what it is that you wish to become accomplished? People will tell you to follow your passion, but you may not be sure where your passion lies Sometimes it's just a matter of trying something and seeing if you have a love for it or not. Does it ignite your passion? Does it unlock hidden potential? This can be a frustrating chase, especially if you are in a career for years and you realize that you have made wrong career path choices. The only choice is to find what inspires you, and follow that passion. You will develop your hidden potential, and once it starts it will become a tidal wave.

You can realize your potential by tapping into three sources – Natural Ability, Education & Training, and Inner Drive.

NATURAL ABILITY

Natural ability is perhaps the easiest one to understand, but also the one that may be the easiest excuse. Some people are just naturally gifted and they were lucky enough to discover their ingrained talents and turn them into a successful profession or hobby. Think of athletes, models, musicians, artists, and numerous others. I previously stated I came to terms with myself that I would not make it as a singer. Frankly, I have a terrible voice for singing. When I was 13, I was thrown out of the church youth choir. The choir director tried to soften the news, like he really didn't think I wanted to sing, but it was obvious my voice was a distraction – didn't blend. Not a problem, it didn't scar me for life. I accept that I do not have the natural voice to be a singer. Actually, neither did Bob Dylan or Willie Nelson, two of my favorite singers. And they seemed to do ok. A good lesson to be learned there. They were both creative songwriters and musical innovators. Realizing they did not have the greatest voice for much of the conventional music of the day, they wrote their own music and style to the point where it not only made their songs top hits, but so unique to them that no other singer could successfully copy. So we all do have natural ability, we may just have to explore a little further to see where it can best fit.

I also acknowledged that I would never play professional basketball. At 5'6" I did not figure there was enough natural ability for that particular profession. Too short to play professional basketball; too tall to be a jockey. So were all my dreams crushed? Of course not, that just eliminated two from thousands of other things I could pursue, have fun at, and possibly be good at. I found that I had the natural ability to be a wrestler, a skier, a distance runner, and a drummer. I've had fun and fulfillment doing all of those. And of course I, like you, have natural abilities to many things that we never pursued. That's ok also, we can't do everything. But if you have a burning desire to do something that is leaving you unfulfilled – then go for it. What's holding you back?

EDUCATION AND TRAINING

The second source for developing potential is education and training. Not a whole lot in life comes naturally, we have to develop skills and abilities. We have the potential to speak several languages. That means we have the potential to learn several languages. No one is born speaking languages, we learn them as we go. So your obligation to yourself is to identify what you desire, then pursue the education and training to get you there.

There are certainly no limits and no excuses for not taking advantage of education and training. Sure it can be expensive, and a serious commitment of your time. You must make the commitment to devote yourself to put the time and effort into whatever training or schooling you select. In today's world there is so much available. There should be something you can find that will accommodate your schedule and budget. We see success stories every day where someone put themselves through college, military training, tech school, or whatever; while raising children and overcoming all sorts of obstacles. You too can make the sacrifice. Plus, it is usually fun and satisfying. There are few feelings of pride and achievement greater than a graduation. That is something you have earned, and will be a better person for it.

Remember, you have so much potential, almost unlimited. So do your children. Take advantage of all the training and education you can. Most businesses offer training in everything from computer skills to public speaking, and all types of job related training. Yet many employees must be forced into participating. How sad, it is your potential the business is trying to develop.

It has always been perplexing to me when experienced people find it insulting to take a training class. They feel they know more than the instructor, who can't possibly teach them anything new. Education cannot hurt. If you feel you already know everything, you can learn how to help others.

Why is it that professional golfers still take lessons? When I was a ski instructor, I enjoyed teaching people, especially beginners. I found it very gratifying. I never had a student who at the end of my first class, was not at least able to control their speed, turn left or right, and stop. And they could do these without fear. Most first session classes also learned how to safely ride the ski lift. But many of my fellow ski instructors preferred intermediate or advanced classes, so they could go on the big mountain. And sometimes the people taking lessons had as much talent and skill as the instructor. They would often be specific, such as saying they just wanted to improve their technique in pole planting; or they were good at aggressively attacking a mogul field, but wanted to be able to take moguls more slowly and with better technique. So to some degree, the experts appreciated their instruction as much as beginners, even if they were as good a skier as their instructor. Musicians are another example. Many expert musicians still routinely take lessons. Again, to pick up a tip on technique, some latest trends, or expand their sound. I have a friend who is an expert guitar player in country and rock, but he took some professional lessons to improve his blues guitar playing.

Everyone has the potential to learn and develop beyond their current level, through education and training.

INNER DRIVE

The third source for realizing your potential is inner drive. We have all marveled at stories where people overcame overwhelming odds and barriers to achieve success. Sometimes it defies medical experts. Some people are so determined that their inner drive pushes them beyond imagination.

"Do you believe in miracles?" was the famous line by broadcaster Al Michaels at the 1980 Winter Olympics, when team USA defeated the Soviet Union. It became known as the Miracle on Ice. A group of USA athletes, mostly college players, got together like an all-star team, and beat the Soviet Union team, which was made up of veteran players who played together for years, comparable to our National Hockey League teams of the time. Yet this group of youth not only beat the Soviet Union, they went on to win the Gold Medal. Yes, they had loads of natural ability, and they went through extensive training, but that night they won on inner drive.

Inner drive is pushing yourself to a new level. Pushing potential you were not even aware you had. How does a runner still manage a new personal best in a highly visible event with other elite runners, when they have practiced this distance thousands of times? How does a figure skater, who never got through the routine without a mistake, go out on the world's biggest stage and nail it flawlessly? It's the inner drive. The "there's no stopping us now" mindset, that we can do our best, and even better. The ultimate will to win. They're as talented as us, they've practiced as hard, we both have a winning game plan, so what will determine the winner? Either by someone making a costly mistake, or someone finding the inner drive to endure and put us over the top.

JOHN A. KELLEY (THE ELDER)

John Kelley was born in West Medford, MA, in 1907, the eldest of ten children. He always enjoyed running and was a miler on the track team in high school. He wanted to run the Boston Marathon, which has been run on Patriot's Day since 1897. He entered his first Boston Marathon at age 20, and did not finish. Four years later he tried it again, and again did not finish. The third time he was doing well but faded near the end to finish 37th. On his fourth attempt he finished second, pretty remarkable. Then in 1935, at age 27, John Kelley won the Boston Marathon. A year later he was leading the race when he started up the fourth of the famous inclines, around mile 20 ½, when he was passed by the eventual winner. He told reporters later that hill just broke his heart, forever giving it the name Heartbreak Hill. Today there is a statue of him at that location.

John never lost his enthusiasm and love for the Boston Marathon. In 1945 he won the race for the second time. He kept coming back again and again. In 1957, at age 50, he finished ninth. Amazingly, that 1957 race was won by John J. Kelley, another great local distance runner, who was no relation to John A. Kelley. That's when the media gave the nicknames for clarity, John J. Kelley "The Younger" and John A. Kelley "The Elder." But John A. Kelley wasn't done yet. I happened to be living in the Boston area in 1992, when then 84 year old John Kelley, finished his 58th Boston Marathon. And he did it with a time of 5:58:36, pretty impressive for an 84 year old. He started the race 61 times, only failing to finish the first two times plus one other time with an injury.

This is a remarkable and inspiring story, but truly shows someone pushing all the limits of their potential. John Kelley certainly had natural ability, he found his passion which blended with his natural gifts. He used education and training, as do all distance runners, to groom their body and mind for the event of the marathon. And lastly, John Kelley showed us inner drive, pushing his own limits in every marathon and training session he encountered. Now ask yourself, are you getting the most out of your potential?

WE'RE BORN TO WIN, THEN CONDITIONED TO LOSE

There is such beauty in youth. They don't have the fears, vanity and intimidations we develop as we age. One time when I was teaching a youth ski school class, one delightful little girl came up to me very puzzled and said "When I grow up, I don't know if I want to go in the Olympics as a ski racer or as an ice skater." It melted my heart. So much unbridled enthusiasm. We're all born winners with no limits on our dreams. I remember saying something like, "you just have fun with both, and maybe you will always be great at both of them, and you will become the first person to compete at both. Or as you get older, one of the sports may become your favorite, but it isn't something you have to worry about now, your job now is to just have fun."

We're born to win. We can do anything we want to be. But then what happens. As stated in Chapter 1, people like our own parents! Teachers, buddies, grandparents, and others who are supposed to love us – start telling us to get real! Come on, it's time to grow up – you can't be a star athlete, a singer, an actress, a doctor, an FBI agent, the President. All of our youthful dreams, and they are starting to pound them down. Telling us what we cannot become.

After a couple years of this, we take the mallet and start pounding ourselves. Who am I kidding? I can't go back to college and get a degree, I can't get promoted to my dream job, I can't start my own business. Too much work and risk to start my own business, too much politics required to be considered for a promotion, too much money and time for more education. Soon we have met the enemy, and it is us. We are now pounding down our own dreams. We have conditioned ourselves to lose. Goodbye dreams. We tell ourselves we have come to reality, as we watch others just like us making the achievements we have given up on. Remember, we are still dealing with potential, so do not be your own worst enemy. Don't let other people do this to you, don't do it to yourself, and for goodness sake, don't do it to your kids.

Chapter 10

Attitude

"Somehow the wires uncrossed.
The tables were turned.
Never knew I had such a lesson to learn.

I'm feeling good from my hat to my shoe.
Know where I'm going and I know what to do.
I've tidied up my point of view. I've got a new attitude.

I'm in control. My worries are few.
Cause I got love like I never knew.
I've got a new attitude."
-sung by Patty LaBelle

Attitude is one of those misused, overused, words thrown around too much that people don't really stop and think about it. I believe most people talk about others who have a negative attitude, but would never consider themselves in that category. We all think our own attitude is great – if only everyone else was positive all the time, like us! Well, when I use the term attitude here as a required ingredient for success, I am not using the nonchalant attitude reference. I am talking the highest levels of self-esteem, confidence, fortitude, determination. You got to feel it, live it, and show it. More than a can-do attitude, I'm talking a deserve-to attitude. You deserve to be successful, you deserve it as much as anyone else. You have to believe that. Either you have earned it, or you're going to earn it. Nothing can stand in your way.

You need to have a strong ego to support this attitude. Some people are afraid of the word ego, like it's a negative connotation. But ego is poise, drive, the will-to-win. Accepting that success comes from your inner self, not from your environment. We make our own breaks. In the chapter on Communications we discussed having to speak or perform in front of others to be successful in any job. It takes ego to do that. And if that is one of your fears, it takes a powerful attitude to overcome the fear of public speaking or entertaining.

Those fears for many people are very real. Look at children. As parents, we may be watching our kids in a swim meet, singing a solo part in a show, saying their lines in a play, or any number of activities. We're just proud of them and enjoy watching them. It really isn't about winning or losing, or getting an award – to us. But the child may be so nervous and stressed out over the event that they have lost all the fun of participating.

I once watched a youth hockey game where a young boy playing defense went to take the puck away from an opposing player in front of his net, and accidently knocked it into his own goal. From the stands, I could hear his own stunned goalie yelling something like "I'm going to kill you." Soon he was on the bench crying uncontrollably while several of his teammates were also yelling at him. The most appalling thing was that the coaches were not interceding. They were ignoring the situation. I felt devastated for the poor kid. This wasn't the Stanley Cup, it was a youth hockey game. I was thinking "remember all the details kid, because you will probably be repeating it to a child psychologist sometime in the future." How do you recover from that bruised ego? Well the thing is, we've probably all had similar moments, and it's all about how you pick yourself up and move forward from there. That's the attitude we need. The coaches should have calmed everyone down, reminded them we're all on the same team, use it as a teachable moment – we learn from those mistakes. And we're going to be a better team and better people supporting each other. Plus, it was one goal, the game was far from over. Most coaches would have said "Don't worry, we'll get it back." Instead it was opportunity lost. And through life we are not always going to have a coach, boss or friend who stands up and supports us. We have to take charge of our own situation and attitude.

BELLA KAROLYI

There have been many great coaches in every sport who were great motivators. A coach has to be a teacher, to prepare and develop their athletes. A coach has to be a planner, to design the winning strategy. Most of all, a coach has to be a motivator, to make their players believe in themselves – to instill the can do/deserve to attitude in the mindset of the individuals and the team.

Perhaps there was no one better at this than Bella Karolyi. Some coaches deal with older, professional athletes; some deal with college or high school age athletes. Bella spent his gymnastics coaching career of close to 40 years teaching and motivating pre-teen and teenage girls. How's that for a challenge? He had many athletes on the world's biggest stages performing at levels most spectators couldn't even fathom.

Going into the 1984 Olympics, no American had ever won a gold medal in gymnastics, and of course the biggest prize was the All-Around. Bella Karolyi was coaching the U.S. team, having defected from Romania. The heavy favorite in the event was his former pupil, Ecaterina Szabo of Romania. Bella was now coaching American Mary Lou Retton. Six weeks before the Olympics, Mary Lou had knee surgery, which doctors announced would take three months of rehab and keep her out of the Olympics. She refused to listen, and her and her coach both demanded that she be allowed to compete. And compete she did, giving her best in every event, and staying within reach of Szabo. It all came down to the final event, the vault. After Szabo finished, it was presumed Szabo had won the gold and Retton would get the silver. Mary Lou was last up. To beat Szabo and win the gold she needed to score a perfect 10. A 9.9 would get her a silver. Now come on, a perfect 10 in Olympic judging, almost non-existent. In fact, the first ever perfect 10 was just accomplished at the 1976 Olympics by Nadia Comaneci of Romania – coached by Bella Karolyi! So he knew how to get the attitude right in his gymnasts.

The rest is history. Mary Lou Retton, with all the ego and confidence in the world, ran to the vault, hit the springboard, went through the air with perfect form, and stuck a perfect landing. She then started jumping and celebrating – before the judges scores went up. Basically giving the message to the judges, "that was perfect and I dare you to give me anything less than a ten." The TV announcer was heard saying "she knows what she has done." Then the scores went up – all tens! That's attitude driving success.

A few Olympics later, in 1996, no U.S. women's gymnastics team had ever won the team gold medal. In fact, Russia had won every gymnastics team gold since 1948, except the one where they boycotted. That one was won by Romania. But in 1996 the U.S. women had an almost dream team, nicknamed The Magnificent Seven. This time, going into the final events of the team competition, the U.S. had a lead over the Russians. Russia would close out with floor exercise, and the U.S. on the vault. Just play it safe, don't make any mistakes, and the U.S. should win the gold. But suddenly, we started making mistakes. First one American fell on her landing, twice; then another gymnast faltered. They were blowing vaults they had done thousands of times. The lead was in jeopardy. The Russians did what they had to do, scoring well on their event, and they were watching, along with everyone else as the final U.S. vaulter, Kerri Strug, came to the line for her first vault. She told herself, this was her moment, she was going to do a vault she has done a thousand times and clinch the gold medal for the team. The worst nightmare happened. Kerri made the jump, great form, then missed the landing. Not only did she fall, but suffered a third degree lateral sprain and tore two ligaments. She was in extreme pain and everyone thought it was all over. The cameras showed her and Bella Karolyi talking, and assumed he was just comforting her. Instead, they were planning her second vault. He told her "Kerri, we need this, and you can do it." Thus unfolded the now famous heroic act, where Kerri Strug managed to run to the vaulting horse, hit the springboard, gracefully fly, twist and flip through the air, and stick the landing on one foot. She held that pose and forced a fake smile long enough to have it score, before she collapsed in pain. Her score, a 9.712, guaranteeing the U.S. women's gymnastics team their first ever gold medal. They wanted her to go immediately to a hospital, but nothing doing. Bella Karolyi carried her to the awards podium where her teammates lifted her on the platform to all accept their gold medals.

Attitude driving success. Whenever you feel you are defeated and ready to give up, think of what advice Bella Karolyi would give to you.

"Some guys have all the luck.
Some guys have all the pain.
Some guys get all the breaks.
Some guys do nothing but complain."- sung by Rod Stewart

This song by Rod Stewart is all about attitude. Some guys have all the luck, and get all the breaks. While some guys have all the pain, and do nothing but complain. Which group are you in? Which group of friends do you find yourself a part of? We've all heard the expression "Misery loves company." Negative people can find such comfort among other negative people. They usually end up trading stories and trying to convince the other person that indeed their situation is worse. What's the goal, to get comfort in piety, or to overcome the situation and become a winner again?

When we're on top and things are going good, it's easy to tell others to have a positive attitude. We sometimes credit our good fortune to our optimistic outlook. Why aren't others positive like me?

I worked with a guy who was on top for many years. Had a good marriage, fine kids, and great family life. Financially they did well, were more than comfortable. He was selected at work for an advanced leadership development program. Everything was wonderful. Then he started to have medical issues. Three years later the doctors still had not diagnosed the cause. He had the finest medical care, and over three years they ran about every type of test anyone heard of. Many several times. They tried numerous medications and therapies, nothing seemed to work. He was suffering constant pain, and was on a number of different pain medications over the span of time. In that period he also needed oral surgery, which did not go well. So in addition to the internal pain and muscle problems, he now had a lot of mouth pain. The dental plate which was made for him caused more pain and affected his speech, so he usually went without it. All these physical problems let to emotional problems, and the doctors recommended that he also see a psychiatrist, who gave counseling and put him on anti-depressants. The next phase of the situation was that it affected his eating and sleeping. He lost his appetite, and many foods would no longer agree with him. Plus, he could no longer get a good night's sleep. Within a six-month period he lost over 40 pounds. He had a very stressful long term assignment on the job, which he took in stride and didn't complain. But he looked terrible as compared to his former self. Two different coworkers approached me to do something. They didn't know what, they were just so worried about him. I met with him a number of times. He wanted to share everything, saying it was good to discuss his frustrations and wanted people to understand – he wasn't doing drugs, not addicted to pain killers, or anything improper. He was just suffering from medical and emotional issues for which no one has yet identified the exact cause or a corrective solution.

I thought things could only get better for him, they could not possibly get any worse. Then they did. His brother committed suicide. When I heard the news I was devastated. I thought that could put anyone over the edge, and in his fragile state, he won't be able to handle it. I reached out to him right away.

Now the question is, how do you tell someone in such a situation to have a positive attitude? If you were in a similar situation and someone told you to stay positive, you'd probably feel like punching them. Sometimes we have to let people grieve, including ourselves. I was close to this person, and he enjoyed talking with me, but I couldn't fathom what all he was going through or how he was going to handle it. He still had his personal issues, now he had to keep the whole family together, including parents and siblings.

But to my absolute amazement, he indeed did keep a positive attitude. He still had confidence in his doctors and kept telling me that all medical problems will get better. The stressful job project was back in control and would soon be ending very successfully. He was relying on a number of good friends for support, and had gotten very close to the crisis pastor at the church, who was helping the family immensely. He made sure his parents and other relatives were all strong, getting the counseling and support they needed, and would all get through the sorrow together.

I admired him and his family so much, how they incredibly stayed strong and together to get through this. He has since recovered from his medical issues. That kind of positive attitude you can't tell someone to have. That just happens, it comes from within. You either have it or you don't. But it does come from training your mind and controlling your environment. Live positive, stay positive, associate with positive friends. Then when crisis happens to you or to others, you are prepared to handle it.

LOU HOLTZ

"I've been on the top in this world and I've been on the bottom, and I'll probably be both places again before I die." - Lou Holtz

Lou Holtz is another of the great coaches who was a teacher and strategy analyst. He was one of the very best at preparing his team emotionally. He made them believers, not only that they could win, but that they deserved to win.

He coached at Notre Dame, where winning is a tradition, so perhaps victory is naturally expected. However, he came to Notre Dame when the program had been struggling for the previous five years. He left after 11 seasons with a record of 100-30-2. The most impressive year was in his third season when the team went 12-0 and won the National Championship. The following year they went 12-1 and finished second.

Prior to Notre Dame he coached two seasons at University of Minnesota. The two years before he became the Minnesota coach their record was 4-18. In his second year they finished with a record of 7-5 and a bowl game, and among their five losses, they lost to Oklahoma by 6, Ohio State by 4, and Michigan State by 5.

Three years after leaving Notre Dame, Lou Holtz decided to come back for one more head coaching assignment. He accepted the position and huge challenge at University of South Carolina. His first season the team went 0-11, which followed the previous year of 1-10. Going into his second year they had a 21-game losing streak. Then followed what has been called the most remarkable turnaround season in the history of Southeast Conference football. They won 17 games over the next two seasons, ranked in the top 20 both years, and both seasons ended with bowl wins over Ohio State.

What is significant in all these examples is that the successful turnarounds occurred in the second and third years. What that indicates, is that the success was achieved with much of the talent that was already there. Most college coaches will say they need several years to recruit their types of athletes, implement their system, and bring cohesion to the coaching staff. But the quick turnarounds led by Lou Holtz show that he took the players who were already there and changed their mindset from being an expected loser into becoming an expected winner. He taught them the "deserve to" attitude. Plus, they had fun doing it. Lou Holtz is a well renowned speaker, humorist and magician. The players enjoyed playing for him; and as a team they were loose, relaxed and confident that they could compete and earn victories against any other team. Attitude driving success.

HIGH SCHOOL SQUANDER

I had several friends in college who had gone to the same high school, and often agonized over this story. Their high school had a good sports tradition, and their football team had always done pretty well. Then during their high school years, the football team was terrible. In their senior season, they won only one game.

This situation is not unusual, and often the coach is the target of the blame. However, the school, players and fans stood by the coach. In fact, the head coach and coaching staff had all been there as a unit for a number of years and had consistent success in the past.

The next excuse in such a situation would be to call it a "building year" or building years. It could have been a period of time where they just didn't have the talent. That is what made this story so incredible – they had some of the best athletes they had seen in years. Many of these teammates had played together since they were little kids, and most followers had predicted championship years when this group got to high school. Here's the most amazing part – among the graduates of a team that won only one game, the following year four players were playing college football. All four saw collegiate playing time in their freshman year.

So how did the team squander such talent? As it turned out, about five years later, their high school won the league championship, and were on top once again. But during the period when most thought they had the best natural talent, the most gifted athletes, they had their worst seasons.

The situation was opposite of the Lou Holtz teams we described. Instead of inspiring players who had low expectations, and converting them to believe in themselves; here we had players and coaches who had the attitude that they were almost assured of victory, and opponents would be afraid of them. They lost respect for their opponents, and probably were thinking more like individual stars instead of congealing as a team. A real attitude failure.

"Connection is what gives purpose and meaning to our life."- Brene Brown

Brene Brown speaks and writes a lot about vulnerability. People have a need to feel connected. Feelings of shame and fear come from feeling disconnected. As stated earlier, despite all the motivating examples of having a positive attitude and believing in yourself, it can be very difficult to make happen. In order to have a "can do/deserve to" attitude about yourself, and a "we can do this" attitude about the team, you have to feel connected, respected and trusted.

She uses the term worthiness. People with a strong sense of love and belonging – believe they are worthy of love and belonging. To get love, respect, and trust from others, you have to give those things to them. This goes both ways. We can't expect a positive connection to come from someone who we don't share with, respect, listen to, or care about. So how do we connect with the great coaches, how do we incorporate this winning attitude?

It all comes back around to confidence, security, ego and belief in yourself. You deserve to be worthy. You deserve to be successful.

Win

When it's all said and done
My once in a lifetime will be back again
Now is the time to take a stand
Here is my chance.

That's why I'll never give up
Never give in
Never let a ray of doubt slip in
And if I fall, I'll never fail
I'll just get up and try again.
- sung by Brian McKnight

Chapter 11

Energy

"When we dream, the things we wish for happen by magic. When we wake, we know without effort a man is less than nothing."- Caine from Kung Fu

The next ingredient is energy, another word with a lot of different implications. In this context we are not referring to physical stamina as much as mental energy. Life has a lot of ups and downs - prosperity and financial stress, good health and bad health, job security and unemployment, happy marriages and bitter divorces, joyous births and sad deaths. We all go through life's ups and downs, and it is draining, especially in mental energy. It takes courage to persevere. Sometimes it takes courage to be sensitive, be honest, take risks, go for opportunities, make change happen, stand up for values and beliefs, show compassion, show your emotions, share your feelings, express your opinion, have an ego. So the kind of energy we are referring to here goes hand in hand with courage – you need courage to exert the energy required to achieve success. Bella Karolyi's gymnasts and Lou Holtz's football players competed in very physically demanding sports. To compete at those levels required a great deal of physical and mental energy, and the courage to let it all out. That's the type of energy required to drive success.

"Success is not final, failure is not fatal. It is the courage to continue that counts."- Winston Churchill

We cannot be afraid of failure. We may have boundless energy, but have a fear of expending it because we might fail. We are not going to win every time. Life would be pretty unfair if we did. At work, many people are in too much fear that they might make a mistake. They may have an intolerable manager who pounces on every mistake. If so, that person should not be in management. No manager can tolerate unlimited careless and costly mistakes; but good managers encourage creative thinking, measurable risks, and support for whatever the outcome.

I used to work in the hospitality industry, an industry which is famous for mistakes. Think of all the comedy movies and television shows where they made fun of desk clerks, waiters, bellboys, maids, and hotel managers, all doing things wrong or treating customers foolishly. Of course the biggest business mistake in history was made in the hotel business. Over 2000 years ago, the hotel manager who didn't give Mary and Joseph a room at the Inn. He told them to sleep in the barn. We don't know if they had reservations, we don't know if the No Vacancy sign was lit, we just know what happened next. We also know that if he had provided excellent customer service and made accommodations, today people would have little hotels under their Christmas trees instead of stables. Opportunity lost.

But like any business, we learn from a mistake and move on. We might have to write a new policy so everyone knows the procedure, train the people better so we don't repeat the mistake, and prepare the options for what to do and say should the situation occur again.

NOLAN RYAN

Nolan Ryan is in the Baseball Hall of Fame, and he holds numerous Major League Baseball records. He was a pitcher who retired with 326 wins. He holds records for most strikeouts – per season, per career. Has the most years with 100 or more strikeouts – 24 years! The most years with 300 or more strikeouts – 15 years! The record he is most famous for is throwing 7 no-hitters. In the long history of baseball, the second best is 4.

At age 44, he had a stress fracture in his back, was taking pain pills and using a heating pad right up to game time. He also had a sore finger and ankle, and almost scratched himself from the lineup. But he discussed it with the coach, and said he would give it a try. Then he went out and pitched his seventh no-hitter. In that game he threw 16 strikeouts, and retired 27 of 29 batters. Except for two walks he would have thrown a perfect game.

But Nolan Ryan holds records that his fans don't talk about, and are kind of humorous. One of the worst things a pitcher can do is throw a wild pitch. He holds the record for the most wild pitches thrown. He led the major leagues in wild pitches six different years. He also gave up more walks than any pitcher in history, and led the major leagues in walks eight different years. He hit the batter with a pitch 158 times, 12th highest in history. He allowed the most grand slams – 10. He made the most errors by a pitcher, in fact he led the league in errors four different years.

Why are these records impressive to me? Because do you think he had a fear of failure? Did it bother him when he threw a wild pitch or allowed a walk, to the point where it took his focus off of his real purpose? Absolutely not. Mistakes, errors, no problem. He had a great sense of humor, and when he made an error or wild pitch, he would just laugh it off and get mentally prepared to strike out the next batter. All focused energy, energy with courage.

JOHN PIERPONT And Son And Grandson

Talk about someone who had the determination to overcome failure. John Pierpont was born into privilege in 1785 in Litchfield, Connecticut. He graduated from Yale University, where his grandfather was one of the founders. For his first career he became a school teacher. However, he was against the discipline tactics required of teachers at the time, and refused to follow the established protocol. Thus, he failed as a teacher.

He went to Litchfield Law School and earned a law degree. However, he failed as a lawyer. He was too generous with his clients, and too concerned about justice to take on high-profile controversial cases which brought in good fees.

He then decided to become a retail merchant and opened a dry goods store. He failed as a businessman. He gave people credit, and would not charge enough for his goods to build profit.

In the meantime, he enjoyed writing poetry, and all the while he would spent his time dabbling in poetry. He was a failure as a poet. Although he did have some works published, he didn't collect enough royalties to make a living in poetry.

He decided he would become a minister, and went to Harvard Divinity School. After graduating, he became an ordained minister at the Hollis Street Church in Boston. Unfortunately, his positions for prohibition and against slavery led to arguments with influential people, and he was forced to resign. Thus, he failed as a minister.

Still believing in himself and wanting to make a difference in society, he turned to his next venture, which was politics. He ran for Governor of Massachusetts as the Abolition Party candidate. He lost. Then he ran for Congress on the Free Soil Party ticket. He lost. Failed as a politician.

The Civil War had started, and he volunteered as Chaplain of the 22nd Regiment of Massachusetts Volunteers. He had to quit after only two weeks because he couldn't keep up with the soldiers. After all, he was now 76 years of age. He couldn't even make it as a Chaplain.

He found a menial job as a file clerk in the back offices of the Treasury Department in Washington, where he worked the last five years of his life. He wasn't very good at that either – his heart was not in it.

John Pierpont died, having accomplished nothing he had set out to do, or to become. Was he a failure? His commitments to social justice, his desire to be a loving person, his active engagement in the great issues of his time, and his faith in people and religion – these are not elements of a failure. After his death, education was reformed, legal processes were improved, credit laws were changed, and slavery was abolished. He was a proud man who stood up for what he believed. That's not being a failure.

There is another contribution John Pierpont made, which still lives on today. Every year around Christmas we celebrate his success. We carry in our hearts and minds a lifelong memorial to him. "Jingle Bells." Remember he was a poet. John Pierpont wrote Jingle Bells. The poem was actually titled A One Horse Open Sleigh. He wrote a poem that stands for the simplest joys, now a song that millions of people around the world know. A song about something few of us have ever done, but can imagine, and we can all sing about it. A Christmas song not about religion or even Santa Claus. Riding through fields of snow in a horse drawn sleigh. A song that everyone of any age can sing the moment the chord is stuck on the piano. One snowy afternoon in deep winter, John Pierpont penned the poem for a program at his church.

We can admire John Pierpont for never giving up. Every failure resulted in determination to try something different. And he left a lasting legacy to the world. Did he expend positive energy, definitely yes. Did he achieve success, yes. Is it without controversy? Whoa-ho, definitely not.

The Son...

One of John Pierpont's sons was James Pierpont. James leaves a tale of his life in a way similar to his father's. James ran away from home at the age of 14, and went from New England to the west coast, where he took a job as a deck hand on a Pacific Ocean ship. He tried his luck in California during the Gold Rush – failure. He tried to establish a photography shop in San Francisco, which was also a failure. He eventually returned to Massachusetts, but later decided to move to Savannah to visit his brother John Jr., who was a rector at a Unitarian Church in Savannah. James had terrific musical aptitude, and became the musical director at the church.

James also opened a retail business in Savannah which sold building and art supplies. Much like his father's mercantile experience, he was also a failure as an entrepreneur.

In 1857 James married the daughter of the mayor of Savannah. James became quite acclimated to Southern life, and was influenced by his wife and father-in-law. When the Civil War started, James enlisted and became a member of the 5th Georgia Volunteer Cavalry, Confederate States Army. He saw hypocrisy in the North's anti-slavery stance since many made money from it. So at the same time his father was trying to be a chaplain in the Union Army, James was a member of the Confederate Army.

James wrote and published several patriotic songs to promote the Confederacy, utilizing his musical talents. After the war, he became a music professor at Quitman Academy.

John Pierpont died in 1866, and James Pierpont died in 1893. In 1857 James copyrighted a song called "One Horse Open Sleigh" which was later changed to "Jingle Bells." It is believed that John wrote the words to Jingle Bells as a poem, then years later James put it to music. Either way, the song was not popular in either of their lifetimes.

The song eventually grew in popularity. The now-famous Christmas song that has no mention of Christmas in the lyrics. As early as 1899 people in Medford, Massachusetts declared Medford as the home of Jingle Bells. Savannah took great exception to this claim, quoting witnesses to the composition of Jingle Bells, naming the owner of the piano and the tavern where it was written. The controversy continues to this day. Both cities have historical markers claiming themselves as the birthplace of Jingle Bells. Most music sheets name James Pierpont as the author since he wrote and published the music – but no agreement as to where.

The Grandson...

So we have a father and son who have dealt with their share of failure and controversy in life, but always found a way to persevere. Could there possibly be a high mark in this family? Third time's the charm? Well, John Pierpont had a daughter named Juliet. Juliet married Junious Spencer Morgan, a financier. They had a son whom they named after his grandfather – John Pierpont Morgan.

Yes, that John Pierpont Morgan. He usually preferred to go by his initials, J.P. Morgan. He became one of the most powerful and wealthiest men in the world. An American financier, banker, philanthropist, art collector, and industrialist. He formed General Electric and U.S. Steel. And of course, J.P. Morgan Bank. He was the grandson of John Pierpont and the nephew of James Pierpont.

They led interesting lives, but those Pierpont's sure left their mark. They had ups and downs, but they never ran out of positive energy.

———————————

Let's bring these illustrations back to our present day work environments. How many times have you, or someone who works for you, tried something that didn't work? Were you fired? Were you thought less of in terms of being a caring, loyal employee? Of course not.

If you try a new venture, a new method, or experiment, whatever – and it doesn't work – you are not a failure. The trial may have been a failure, but not the people who developed a concept and took a chance. That's how we discover greatness.

Whenever something doesn't work, if it creates a fear of trying again, then there is a failure. But if it is an inspiring experience – we got so close, next time we might get it – that is a success.

It doesn't matter if it is a wild pitch, or a career failure where we have to go back to school and start something else totally new – the energy that is spent moving forward towards the new objective, is the positive energy and attitude that achieves success.

Chapter 12

Values

"Do the right thing. It will gratify some people and astonish the rest." - Mark Twain

We now have three elements critical for achieving personal success – potential, attitude and energy. We still need one more – values. Can someone be successful without values and ethics? Not if we apply the proper description of success.

Look at evil mobsters. We can take the real life John Gatti or the fictional Tony Soprano. Both definitely had potential to achieve great things. They certainly had an ego-driven positive attitude that they could accomplish what they wanted. And they surely had focused energy with courage.

What they did not have were values. Without values people become misguided, and doomed for failure. Values are an individual thing, you mold your own. We are not born with values, they are developed. Values are formed from our experiences and learned from teachings. As we grow through life's experiences and influences, we form our own set of values. But don't blame your past, your teachers, your parents, or any other influences for bad values. We all have our own moral compass of right from wrong, and we all have horrible events in our past that we could use for a cop out of our values. There is simply no excuse for having a low standard for our personal values.

It always puzzles me how a person can be active in church, coach little league, participate in charities, be a solid citizen – then put on a suit, go to the office, and make unethical business dealings, violate environmental laws, and show discrimination among employees. We should not do that stuff. Not because we may get into trouble, or because it's against policy. We shouldn't do it because it goes against our values.

We can teach a child not to fight – a right/wrong value. We can teach children manners – values. But if we send mixed messages, bad examples, how can we expect them to accept and believe in the values we are preaching. Thus, why do business leaders so often violate the values they expect their people to uphold?

We must all make difficult business decisions. That's leadership. But difficult decisions are different than unethical decisions. And if you think you can't tell the difference you are not being honest with yourself. We have to stand up for our values. We send men and women in uniform to risk their lives to protect the values we hold dear as a nation. So do not make a bad business decision or judgement which could hurt you or someone else, or the company, if in your heart you know it is wrong.

LEFT BRAIN / RIGHT BRAIN

We want to use our own mind and our own thoughts to apply our talents and values as an individual. We have all heard the explanations of left brain / right brain.

Left brain is where we draw on facts, figures, format, analysis, controls, structure, systems and procedures. Right brain is where we draw on feelings, emotions, fantasy, creativity, innovation, artistic talents. We all have a brain and we all have both sides. All of our brains have more potential than we will ever use. But we have also been programmed by our lifetime of influences – our parents, schools, churches, society.

So what happens when we have a problem: "I lost my wallet; I forgot my homework; I left the book at home; I must exchange this but I lost the receipt; I didn't realize what time it was; it's past the deadline to sign up; my shirt got torn; I feel embarrassed; I'm being picked on?"

You want compassion, understanding, sympathy, friendship, support, and help. We've all been in these situations, and we've seen others in these predicaments. The victim is in right brain emotions and needs right brain caring: "I'm sorry for your inconvenience; let me help you; I know how you must feel."

But what is the programmed response we usually get – left brain! From teachers, store clerks, coaches, parents, even friends: "That's not my problem; you understood the rules; it's our policy; it's past the deadline; we can't give refunds; if we allowed an exception for you we'd have to do it for everyone!"

We've all been on both sides of these situations. We say "Don't blame me, blame the system." That's the easy way out. But is that showing compassion and caring; is that living with your values? Enlightenment takes courage. Challenging the system with your feelings of what's right – takes courage.

Values means knowing right from wrong, and doing what is right. Helping others, giving back, being grateful, saying thank you, giving others credit. Standing up for your values means defending the wrongly accused, the abused, and the bullied. Standing up to peer pressure. It takes courage.

WORKING FOR THE MOB

I've already used a mob analogy, but I have a closer tie to the experience. The two worst years of my career. I was offered a position as vice president of Human Resources for a private holding company, which appeared to be a pretty impressive business conglomeration. Several lines of businesses which all catered to the public, and had beautiful buildings and facilities. I did get some red flag warnings from a friend, which I brought up in the interview process. I told them I heard they had a terrible reputation as a place to work. Very smoothly, the response was that's why they needed me. They told me they had changed their ways, and turned over the bad management, but needed someone like me to restore best business and people practices and get their good reputation back. All lies, but it sounded good and I accepted the challenge. The business had 4000 employees yet several entities were registered as a single proprietorship, together the largest single proprietorship in the country. It didn't take long to observe there were a lot of unethical business practices. In fact, it didn't take too long to observe there were a lot of highly illegal business practices. And it appeared obvious and was openly discussed among the workforce – everyone seemed to be aware of it. I was also getting suggestions from trusted people inside the company to keep copies and files at home. Several told me, "We all make copies and keep files at our homes for protection." Not something you want to hear soon after you join a new company. It was a big job, I had fourteen human resources directors reporting to me. Yet at the executive level, the chief financial officer and I were the only two who were "outsiders." All of the other members of senior management were not only of a certain nationality, but most had moved here from their home country. Most people in the company, other than senior positions, referred to the place as the mob. Let me make it clear, the improper practices were all in the financial, discrimination, retaliation, categories – white collar crimes. There were no physical or property violence types of incidents.

Needless to say, it was a horrible experience. I cared too much about values, ethics and people to continue with the company. One evening the chief financial officer and I were discussing the terrible business practices and treatment of people, both inside and outside the company, and realized that most policies had either his name or my name on them. We jokingly said that one evening on the news they might show the place being raided, and the two guys in handcuffs with trench coats over their heads would be him and me. So we both decided to look for new jobs.

A few years later I attended a high school reunion for my wife's high school. I was talking with another husband of a classmate of my wife, and we were discussing all the places we had lived. We both had moved around a lot, but had one city in common. He remarked that we both lived in that particular city, what years were you there? Same time. Who did you work for? Here is where I usually got concerned.

Either people didn't hear of the holding company's name, although they were familiar with their retail operations; or if they were familiar with the company name there would often be an argument – because they had conducted so many unethical business dealings.

So I reluctantly said that you probably have not heard of the company, it is a private business, and said the name. When he froze and appeared speechless, I knew he was familiar. He then asked what my position was, and I told him. He asked if I knew the owner, and if I was ever in his office. I said he was my boss, and of course I was in his office, and was once in his vacation home. He was clearly upset, and wished we could have met at a class reunion a few years earlier. He then said, "You didn't ask me what I do for a living." With that he showed me his badge as an FBI agent. He had been on assignment under a dummy company which was an FBI task force to get this guy. And he said the one thing they were looking for was an inside person who could wear a wire. I would have been ideal for the role. I was taking this somewhat lightly, and said that people in the company jokingly used to call the company the ****** mob. He seriously responded that the FBI doesn't joke about such things, and the FBI also referred to them as the ****** mob. I said "you mean I was a vice president for the mob – that's going to look good on my resume!"

As far out as that story might seem, a similar thing happened to another acquaintance of mine, who had originally been brought to our firm as an outplacement client. He was a chief financial officer, and landed a new position. When he came in to see me about two years later, he had an incredible story to tell. He had left the first company where he had been hired, and went with a larger international organization. He said the company was big, had very nice offices, and he enjoyed his work, which was mostly in mergers and acquisitions. There was a lot of travel to some other cities where the company had offices, but he had never observed or heard talk of any improper transactions. Then one day the offices were raided by the FBI, who burst into the office with guns drawn and screaming for everyone to freeze, and do not touch any computers or phones. Just like in a movie, there were dozens of agents, all dressed in black with FBI logo. They came in with carts and confiscated every computer in the office. There were trucks outside to load the computers and file cabinets that were taken. He said over the next nine months he had been interrogated several times, but honestly never knew of or suspected any wrongdoing. But the business was an arm of the ****** mafia (different country name than mine). So these things actually do happen, thankfully rarely.

I purposely left out a lot of details and names, for obvious reasons. But in terms of values, I think I have seen some of the worst. When government or our legal systems fail, you would like to think that businesses would adhere to their own standards of values and ethics and do what is right, but unfortunately it doesn't always work that way.

The other lesson to pass along is to always do your homework when looking into a new company for a job, and especially when dealing with new ventures or partnerships. There are countless stories of people being cheated out of money, or set up to face a criminal violation, by an unscrupulous business partner. They may not be as extreme as a criminal element, but their business ethics and the way they treat people, both inside and outside the company, should be key warning signs to thoroughly research before you get involved.

THE WHOLE NINE YARDS

Let's go to an analogy a little more on the lighter side. For years I've heard the expression used in various context "the whole nine yards." I started asking people who used it what that exactly meant. I got many responses. Some said it is from football. Then I explained that in football you need ten yards for a first down, nine yards comes up a yard short. So what good is the whole nine? Some said it has something to do with horse racing. Again, the tie in to nine yards falls apart. Some say it has something to do with sewing and fabrics. Nope.

The expression actually refers to cubic yards. In cement trucks. Most ready-mix cement trucks have a capacity of eight to ten cubic yards, and nine is the usual standard. Years ago it was a somewhat common practice for a cement truck driver to sell little side jobs. He may have been running many trips, along with other drivers, to a major pour. On the way he would stop for a job where they had their forms all in place to repair a step or sidewalk, and only needed a small amount like a yard or less. So the driver would take the little cash deal, then proceed to the big job where no one would notice a yard short. Thus came the expression, "Be sure we get the whole nine yards."

Well, there were two partners who had a very successful cement business. They would usually underbid their competition, and promised their drivers were all honest and never did side jobs. Their secret, which only the two of them knew, was that they would short every truck by a half yard of cement before it left their yard. Hands on quality control – they were the ones who filled the trucks.

This system served them well for years, and they both enjoyed the prosperity their business brought them. Both had nice families, impressive homes, boats, living the dream. Then something happened. One partner's daughter asked her father to participate in a program with her at church. He got involved and started getting active with the whole family at church. After a few months, the experience changed his complete outlook. He explained to his partner that ever since he started getting active in the church his whole family is closer, he has an interest in community and civic involvement, they all participate in church activities together, they talk more and are more open with each other, really has improved their life.

His partner said wow that sounds great, maybe I'll start going to this church too. The first guy said, no, you can't go to church too – who's going to measure the cement?

———————————————

As we said, values are developed. We are all a product of our environment and experiences. While some values are carved in stone, with others we must remain flexible, and continue to question and evaluate. With the ever changing dynamics like technology and terrorism, we indeed have laws, ethics and values that no one would have even thought were needed just a short time ago.

That's why I always say that a good Human Resources policy is one which will provide a guideline on how to handle a particular situation about 95 to 98% of the time. You should always allow a little room for common sense to prevail when necessary.

I have a short test for evaluating changes and new concepts. Fortunately, people frequently come to me with suggestions and recommendations. My quick screen to determine if we should move forward consists of three questions. Is it good for the company? Is it good for the people? Is it cost justified? If all three are a yes, it's a no-brainer, a win-win-win. If any two of the three are yes, it warrants further consideration. If any two are no, the suggestion is rejected. This is a quick logical check as well as a values check.

I also frequently get questions from employees asking what the law on a particular issue is. Some people think there is a law for everything, when quite often there is not. However, more and more often there are legislative changes coming into effect in different state or municipal areas which make it an ongoing task to keep up with.

I usually answer the employee's concern with the explanation that there are laws, and policies, and past precedence. First and foremost, we do comply with all workplace laws. There is no excuse for ignorance, we must be aware of applicable laws and remain in compliance. Often when there is no law, there may still be legal requirements as to how the situation is handled. For example, someone may ask how much paid vacation time the company is required to give me by law. The answer is the law doesn't require that you are given paid vacation time. May have a hard time attracting and retaining quality employees, but it is not required by law. But then there is a big "however" that comes into effect. However, if the company does choose to give paid vacation, they cannot discriminate within an employee classification. So they can't give me one week, and my coworker two weeks, and another worker three weeks – if it is based on a discriminatory practice. Based on length of service, fine. Terms of a job offer – fine. Based on gender, age, race, etc. – illegal.

So we obey all laws. Next, where there is no particular law, we get into company policy. Again, exceptions can be made for certain circumstances, and should be documented accordingly. However, the applicable circumstances cannot be discriminatory.

In areas where there are no laws or policies governing the situation, we look at past practices. If the situation came up ten times and was handled ten different ways, there is no particular past precedence. However, if it was handled in a particular consistent manner the previous nine times and you are number ten, and receive adverse treatment, you may have a case for a discriminatory practice.

The point is, values of fairness and proper treatment should always rule. Violations of laws, policies and even past precedence can all be enforceable factors in a court of law if handled with discriminatory practices.

Many decisions and opinions today are based on our constitution, as argumentative as that may be. I'm all for the constitution, but it has been interpreted in some questionable ways. Some of our smartest minds try to read the minds of people who wrote the constitution well over 200 years ago. It really cracked me up when I was listening to a debate about freedom of speech and censorship on the internet, when someone was asked to interpret the intent of the Founding Fathers. Trust me, with all the problems they tried to solve, and as visionary as they were, our Founding Fathers did not discuss the internet.

Our Founding Fathers are cherished and respected. We speak of them almost with reverence. They were the most brilliant men of their time. By invitation, we gathered the best people throughout the colonies. 55 men came to Philadelphia to draft our constitution. They were brave, honest, educated, religious people. They had great vision. If they walked among us today, they would likely be highly educated people in leadership positions. They were among our best people of their time. They had values which were proper, for their time. Or did they?

Indeed they were great men. Yet these great, visionary people, who started a country with the motto "In God We Trust" and granted everyone "Life, Liberty and the Pursuit of Happiness," did not give women the right to vote or own property. They started a country based on the premise that "All Men Are Created Equal," yet thirteen of the men who penned those words owned human slaves. We know they were good people; we don't hate them, we're not ashamed of them. We accept that they were a product of their times, their upbringing, their culture, and their environment.

We have to base our values on the real world as it exists today. The world and our society are changing fast. Some values can become outdated.

"Be who you are and say what you feel, because those who mind don't matter, and those who matter don't mind."- Dr. Seuss

Values are personal, and they are yours. If your values are wholesome and proper, they will define you. If you are sincere and live by honorable values, you will be respected. The choices you have to make to live by your values should not be difficult. You should not have a hard time resisting the influence of others if they want you to go against your values.

The International Institute for Quality and Ethics in Service and Tourism developed a seven-question ethics test to apply when wrestling with decisions that may compromise your values:

1.Is it legal?
2.Am I hurting anyone?
3.Is it fair?
4.Is it honest?
5.Does it bother my conscience?
6.Would I publicize my decision?
7.What if everyone did it?

Good questions to apply to your personal values. It actually makes decisions easier.

Now you have the four ingredients to personal success – potential, attitude, energy and values. If you possess all four and use them wisely, there are no other barriers in your way.

Chapter 13

Individual Contributor to
Dynamic Leader

*"The conductor of an orchestra doesn't make a sound. He depends
for his power on his ability to make others more powerful." -
Benjamin Zander*

INDIVIDUAL CONTRIBUTOR

The transition of going from an individual contributor, a role in
which you do not supervise others, to a supervisor, can be an
interesting experience. Everyone probably remembers the first time
they became responsible for the work of someone else. Some of us
were trained and coached for the transition. Others may have been
given minimal or even zero guidance. Some may have considered this
as achieving one of their major career goals; and others may have been
scared to death.

Look at the circumstances that come into play. Some people have
been more than ready, and perhaps deserved this promotion a long time
ago. Whereas some may have been reluctantly thrown into a position
for which they were unprepared, and faced with peer resentment. No

matter what the situation, if you now have the role and responsibility, you better grow into it. That doesn't mean everyone will eventually have supervision as part of their job. Many people do not want it or need it.

Most people start out their career as an individual contributor, reporting to a more experienced "boss" from whom they will learn their job skills. They perform their job requirements, improving and expanding their abilities as they gain more experience. They may move from that position to any of several other individual contributor positions in their function.

Simple advice: enjoy your job and do it well. Take full advantage of the learning opportunities to gain experience and knowledge. As you grow in this job you will find the motivation for which direction you want to take your career. Remember, not everyone is a ladder climber; so don't feel pressure brought onto you by others who are "coaching" your career. Many people enjoy their job, find it satisfying and fulfilling, and are more than content in continuing to do just that for a long time.

CAREER PROFESSIONAL

There are countless successful career paths which will always remain in the category of individual contributor. There are doctors, engineers, artists of every type, lawyers, sales people, professors, consultants, and many others who will always be individual contributors. If the definition of management is getting work done through other people; well, these people get work done by doing it themselves. And that's just the way they like it. They can take their accomplishments to great heights, achieve wealth and recognition, while enjoying their chosen profession.

In speaking with numerous people in this category, one of the things they enjoy most is the fact that they do not have to deal with managing other people. They would not want to be responsible for the work of others, for disciplining people in matters of work rules or personality issues, for doing performance appraisals, or any of the other hassles of managing subordinates. They get to follow their passion doing the work they enjoy and do well.

As companies continue to grow, the more of these professional opportunities there are. In every discipline, there are positions at every level, which do not manage others. Indeed, the business operations, sales and marketing, research and development, corporate support services, all need more people to do the work. Over the years, due both to economic downsizing as well as the progression of information through computer systems, many companies have increased their need for career professionals and less need for middle managers. And since career professionals exist at all levels, one can fulfill a career eventually rising through higher levels of their discipline.

FIRST TIME SUPERVISORS

No matter how the opportunity was handled, if you find yourself as an entry level supervisor, there are a lot of skills to be developed. There are many procedures required to supervise other people, which may be in place by past precedence, company policies, or workplace laws. And as a supervisor, you are accountable. Hopefully you are in a company that provides the necessary training and support. There are many employers that do not, thus you may be on your own. That's dangerous in itself, because if different managers are handling situations in an inconsistent manner, that could get the company in trouble.

In addition to learning the rules, forms, systems and policies, the first-time supervisor must start developing people skills. If you were one of the crew last year, and now you are their boss, you are in a vulnerable situation which takes skill in how to handle. Your old coworkers will try to manipulate you into granting them favors, or special treatment, or sharing confidential information. They will accuse you of showing favoritism. They may guilt you by reminding you that you used to be one of the gang, and now you are one of those management types. I always advise people to be aware of this manipulation, and throw the guilt back on them. Say something like, "You know this is my job responsibility now, and if you are my friend, you wouldn't ask me to do that." It's not always easy, but you must respect your own role, and you will learn the skills of how to handle it.

Also for the first time, you are now expected to be a teacher and motivator. To succeed in this role you must be unselfish, and have a sense of compassion and fairness.

MIDDLE MANAGEMENT

Despite the elimination of layers of middle management positions through the economic restructuring era, this is still a big world. For many people, middle management is the achievement of their goal, and they are happy to spend the rest of their career in their rewarding job. They made it to a prestigious position, are well suited and satisfied with this position, and do not have the qualifications or interest in going any higher up the corporate ladder. They are at a good salary level, can handle the job, and are quite content.

That doesn't mean you can turn off your enthusiasm. To remain successful and valued in the job you must still remain on a course of continuous learning. There are always changes and trends in every discipline, and to remain relevant, you must have a passion for staying current. Likewise, your people will be changing and many will look to you to help them with their goals and aspirations. The worst thing you can do is hold good people back. Encourage them and do everything you can to help them advance. Better to lose good people to opportunities within the company than to lose them to outside competition. Plus, a big part of your job success will be measured on how good you develop people.

There are of course many available avenues for movement within the middle management levels, both vertically and laterally. There are many technical skills to be learned for every discipline. While you don't have to be the best craftsperson at every job, you must learn enough to understand and manage the function. However, you do have to know the administrative skills, like planning and reporting; and the interpersonal and communication skills to keep motivation and harmony in your department.

It is referred to as middle management for a reason. You are responsible for an important part of the business production and the people who report to you. Plus, you have the responsibility to furnish information, and make presentations, to the levels above you. You must depend on your people, and they depend on you. This is what makes a valuable middle manager – when their people are happy and productive, and they provide the best service to their customers and the company.

SMALL BUSINESS OWNER

Dynamic leadership doesn't only exist in large corporations. It can exist in businesses of all sizes. It can also exist in the world of the Entrepreneur. Indeed, some examples of very dynamic leaders are in the owners of small businesses.

When we ran our consulting company, most of our clients were small business owners. I have worked with a wide range of good to not so good. But I will focus on the good. First, they were usually the founders of the business, so they had a great deal of pride and passion for their mission. They had a partnership with their customers that was different in some ways than that found in corporations. They were playing with their own money, and the loyalty they showed key customers was very sincere.

Since they were entrepreneurs, their major fulfillment was dealing with their products and their customers. They did not want to get sidetracked with the problems of financial controls, computer systems, marketing, people issues, facility maintenance, and so on. Their focus was on their passion and growth. This is why they hired consultants like us.

The successful ones seemed to have a natural way with people. The attitude shown towards employees was one of commitment and mutual appreciation. They had the highest standards of quality, and instilled this in their workforce. They enjoyed teaching and developing key people.

They also showed a sense of self awareness, for where their business fit. They did not compete with the giants of industry, but keenly targeted a niche for where they could excel. They also knew their limits. They did not want to become one of the giants, but executed their growth into their market niche very deliberately and without risking the house.

FAMILY BUSINESS

There is a difference between a small business owner and that of a family business. I had some of each as clients. By family business I mean at least a second generation of family ownership, and one which generally has a number of family members working in the business. Two of my clients had over 100 years in business, and were in the fifth generation of family management. Turnover tends to be lower among family members, and tenure is usually longer than in other companies.

Some family businesses are small, and have most of the workforce coming from the family. Others, such as the two I made reference to, have several hundred employees, and most of the key management is from the family.

Does this always make for harmony? Of course not. Obviously, there can be natural resentment from the non-family workers. But for the most part, the workforce did accept them and also respected them. Many family members were well experienced in the business, often starting with summer jobs while still in high school. And most, especially those designated for future leadership positions, were well educated, many attending some of the country's finest business schools. They also showed sincere appreciation for their workers, and treated them well. Perhaps because there wasn't the element of competition seen in non-family businesses.

One day I was in the shipping area of a large distribution company. A high school aged girl was helping pack boxes. They were all very friendly and happy to be teaching her all the elements of their jobs. These were mostly middle-aged men, and one of them said to me "She's a great kid, and she'll probably be our boss one day." There was clearly no resentment; they actually seemed proud that they were helping her to develop into a future leader.

I've seen family owned and operated companies in a variety of industries, and it was generally the same – the family leadership actually tried to create a family type atmosphere among all employees, and most employees had admiration for the royal family. Family businesses also seemed to become much more involved with the community, from civic events to charity support. This was another source of pride for the workforce.

SENIOR MANAGEMENT

Executives. This is the category most people hold in either esteem or contempt. The ones held in high esteem by both their peers and the workforce are the leaders we try to emulate. They are inspirational with people and have a business acumen that impresses their own company stakeholders as well as the competition. Yes, the good ones are well known among the competition.

Admirable senior management also earned their way to their level and built a network of support along the way. Thus, there is no resentment for their success, only a sincere enthusiasm from people who want to be part of their inner circle. These leaders not only earned their role, but they work very hard to continue earning the trust and support of those they serve. They look at their leadership as service (remember servant leadership style).

What about those viewed with contempt? How did they get there, and how do they keep their position? Often they did not earn their level. Rather, it may have been appointed by favoritism or from them taking credit for the work of others. Regardless, some people can grow into the position when given a great opportunity. However, this type generally has an ego that they deserved this position, and are better than those below them. They do not sincerely care for their subordinates, other than the ones who pledge their loyalty. They generally have an insecurity spurned by the fact they know they are not prepared for their responsibility, or liked by people they should be dependent upon. As a result, they have a lack of trust for others. One would think that their situation would not be sustainable and resolve itself, yet I have witnessed people with this description last many years, and hurt the careers or drive away many talented people. They may be too politically entrenched or connected for whatever reason, for the company to take the action they know they should. Now we are referring to action at the CEO/Board level.

How do some become so admired, while others are disrespected? It's not always a misplacement. Like any job, some people succeed at what they do, but are not material for the next level. And some excel at the next level, even if their promotion was a stretch – they may not have been the most qualified candidate. The best producer does not always make the best manager.

The best player does not always make the best coach. Two of the people I have always greatly admired, are Wayne Gretzky and Joe Paterno. We even had a dog named Gretzky JoPaw. Both were famous players and coaches. But one is remembered more for being a great player; the other is remembered more for being a great coach.

DISTRIBUTED LEADERSHIP

Everyone admires a dynamic leader. We know one when we see one. And they can exist in any of the previous seven categories covered. As Ben Zander would say, "You can lead from any chair." We all have the autonomy and accountability to do the right thing, stand up to injustice, and bring to light any predictable bad outcomes we see about to happen. It may be acceptable by a person's role to voice no objection, let a disaster happen, and have others (especially the responsible executive) take the blame. "That wasn't my job, nobody asked me what I thought." Well, that is a standard of behavior that has no place in any business.

Distributed leadership is an approach in which collaboration occurs between people who trust and respect each other's opinions. It succeeds where there is an organizational culture of openness and inclusion across the organization, and is most effective when people at all levels engage and share with a sense of equality and acceptance.

The advantage of an employee-owned company is that every person realizes they have that implied responsibility – to speak up when they see something that isn't right, or voice concern when they see a pending problem. This same commitment exists in family-owned businesses by those in the family, regardless of position. However, most people do not work in an employee or family owned business. And to be a dynamic leader or even a dynamic contributor, you must have this mindset – that your job is an important part of the business, and you have a responsibility to the overall success of the business. If you are frustrated with your job or feel there are limited growth opportunities, trust me, that mindset will get you noticed.

Chapter 14

Inspiring Team Excellence

Teamwork
- Edgar Albert Guest

It's all very well to have courage and skill
And it's fine to be counted a star.
But the single deed with its touch of thrill
Doesn't tell the man you are.
For there's no lone hand in the game we play,
We must work to a bigger scheme.
And the thing that counts in the world today
Is how do you pull with the team?

They may sound your praise and call you great,
They may single you out for fame.
But you must work with your running mate
Or you'll never win the game.
Oh, never the work of life is done
By the man with a selfish dream.
For the battle is lost or the battle is won
By the spirit of the team.

You may think it fine to be praised for skill,
But a greater thing to do
Is to set your mind and set your will
On the goal that's just in view.
It's helping your fellow man to score
When his chances hopeless seem.
Its forgetting self till the game is o're
And fighting for the team.

So we've finally reached the identity of Dynamic Leader. Next question is "Leader of what?" And the answer is of course, a team. What is a team? As we said before, it can be a business team, a sports team, a committee, a department, a task force, or any similar group brought together for a common purpose. A team can be long-term entity or a short-term project function.

Definitions of teams are found everywhere. Here are three I've come across in business articles:

1.A group of people with different skills and different tasks, who work together on a common project, service, or goal, with a meshing of functions and mutual support.

2.A group of people with a full set of complementary skills required to complete a task, job or project. Team members operate with a high degree of interdependence, share authority and responsibility for self-management, are accountable for the collective performance, and work toward a common goal and shared rewards.

3.A team is any group of people organized to work together interdependently and cooperatively to meet the needs of their customers by accomplishing a purpose and goals.

Confusing? Not really. The point is there are really no rules – a team can be comprised of any group of people, whether they have common skills or not. They can be a team of common expertise, or a cross-functional team. What is most important is that they have a common understanding of their mission and purpose.

Just as there are no rules for defining a team, there is not one formula for a successful team leader. Everyone is different, teams are different. There is a lot of room and opportunity for individual styles in inspiring a team.

A dynamic leader, at any level, can be the leader of a team. And whatever their title, they have the responsibility to coach, instruct, inspire and motivate the drive to succeed – together. Leading a team does not come with a script and checklist. It is individualized, based in a large part on experience and judgment.

The team leader must collaborate, to bring out the best of every team member. If successful, the team together is greater than the sum of all its parts. The strength of each individual, when joined, is superseded by a dynamic team. Of course, that is not easy to accomplish. The most successful team leaders are those that can assemble and drive a team with full participation and collaboration.

Teams don't just happen, and some may not buy into the team concept. The biggest challenge may be to engage all members, and be prepared to deal with any resistors. I have had many discussions with such people. They would make statements like "I just want to do my job and be left alone. I don't need to be anybody's friend." I would usually tell them to please do themselves and everyone else a favor, and find somewhere else to earn their living. I want so much more than that from our people. Their attitude does not fit with the workplace culture and atmosphere we want to have.

Teams are groups of two or more people who interact and influence each other, are mutually accountable for achieving common objectives and perceive themselves as a social entity within an organization. Even one person who resists being a team participant can provide a negative impact on the team as a whole. All teams exist to fulfill some purpose, such as assembling a product, providing a service, operating machinery, planning an event, preparing a proposal, or making an important decision. Team members are held together by their interdependence and need for collaboration to achieve a common goal.

A team can be any size. When you are a member of a team, and we are all part of many, you have your share of responsibility to contribute and keep the team going. If you are one of twenty people on a team, you have one-twentieth of the responsibility. If you are on a two-person team, you have 50% of the responsibility. Yes, a team can be comprised of just two people. There are many successful two-person teams. What would country music be without them?

TEAM LEADERSHIP STYLES

Going back to communication styles, the leader of a team can be successful regardless of their personal style. However, it behooves team members to be aware of their leader's style so as to understand and contribute in harmony.

Dominant Leader: A dominant leader will exhibit determination and confidence. They will make a decision, stand by it, and get everyone into the action. A dominant leader will keep the group focused and on task to meet the deadline. Winston Churchill, who led England through World War II is an example of a dominant leader.

Expressive Leader: Expressive leaders lead by keeping everyone engaged and enlightened. Their enthusiasm is contagious. All team members will share in the vision. Expressive leaders will keep the group motivated. Jack Welch, former head of General Electric, is an example of an expressive leader.

Analytical Leader: They will make decisions based on facts and data, and ensure team members have done proper research and analysis. They lead by the knowledge that the group is prepared, informed, and ready to take on the project. Analytical leaders are thorough planners, and are accurate, industrious and prudent. Steve Jobs, former head of Apple, is an example of an analytical leader.

Amiable Leader: Those who lead through collaboration, compromise and participation of all team members. They put the team before themselves. Amiable Leaders are supportive, patient, respectful, cooperative and loyal to the team. President Barack Obama, who modeled Abraham Lincoln's Team of Rivals concept, is an example of an amiable leader.

SPORTS TEAMS

There are numerous team sports, with many championships every year. It takes great team dynamics to win a championship, at any level. A championship requires good coaching, mental preparation, conditioning, game plans, and practicing the fundamentals.

Occasionally there is a dynasty – labeled when a team repeatedly wins championships over several years. Each year, somebody has to win, but how does a team win repeatedly and establish a dynasty? Especially in today's environment where there is frequent turnover. School and college teams have limited eligibility – players graduate or leave school and turn professional. In professional sports, players turn free agent, and move on for higher salaries. Some are traded, and some retire. Coaches and General Managers, at the college and professional levels, continually recruit to find new talent.

It's hard to get to the top, even harder to stay at the top. So to build a dynasty, you have to instill a winning culture – one that will remain even as the players change. When you see a dynasty, the team excellence is alive in the athletes, the ownership, and the fans. And it remains even as players change, sometimes even as coaches change.

NASCAR

Auto racing at the highest levels, both NASCAR and open wheel, is a team sport. The top drivers are celebrities, and win all of the accolades. Yet when interviewed, the credit is always about the team. "We" had a good strategy today. "We" took a risk on the last pit stop. The team is comprised of the crew chief, the pit crew, the owners, and dozens of employees back at the shop who are building engines and chassis. In that particular sport, the team concept also extends through sponsors and suppliers, where there is true interdependence on each other.

UNDER ARMOUR

Kevin Plank is the charismatic CEO of Under Armour. He played college football at University of Maryland, and saw a need for a new product. Football players everywhere wore cotton tee shirts under the pads, which would get wet, hot and heavy from sweat. His idea was simple, make the undershirts out of a material which would stay cool and dry. He had started a business as a student called Cupid's Valentine, which sold roses for Valentine's Day. That was so successful, he invested $17,000 from his flower business to start his new company, Under Armour. He researched fabrics and after a lot of trial and error, had what he felt was the right product, and began operations – in the basement of his grandmother's home. Today Under Armour is a multi-billion dollar business with several thousand employees, and growing. Kevin had the confidence and audacity to enter the sports apparel business, dominated by established companies like Nike, Adidas, Reebok, and many others. In a few years the company has become a major player, and continues to broaden their product line.

Most every element of their business is designed around the team concept. Their marketing is always about teams, not the individual. Their target customers are team sales, which has been the basis of their skyrocketing success. The management style and the way business is conducted, all has a teamwork focus.

One example is the way meetings are conducted. Anyone who has ever worked for a large company has observed the vast number of meetings occurring daily – some productive, some a waste of time and money. At Under Armour they use fast-paced huddle meetings. These can be planned or impromptu. Can be in a conference room or just gather in a circle. There are six rules for the meetings, which are taught to employees (note the sports team jargon and effectiveness):

1. Be prepared to huddle.
2. Manage the clock.
3. Know your position.
4. Run the huddle.
5. Execute the play.
6. Respect your teammates.

TEAM DYNAMICS

Success in any organization is based upon its employees and their ability to work together as a team. This does not just happen organically, it takes a conscious effort to get individuals at various levels with divergent personalities and skill sets to operate cohesively.

Michael Olguin has developed seven recommendations for generating a successful team dynamic.

1.Create a "We" culture. A team culture starts at the top. Senior executives must encourage an environment where the whole organization speaks in "we" references as opposed to "I" reference. The whole organization is serving employees and clients, not just specific individuals. This must be reflected at every level.

2.Clearly define roles and personal growth plans. When people know what their role and responsibilities are, there is far less competitiveness in an organization. This allows employees to come together as a team in an environment where everyone can contribute creatively and strategically. When employees understand what expectations are available for them to progress to the next level, they are more apt to be a good team player. They understand that they are preparing themselves, and not competing with their colleagues, for success.

3.Recognize success, regardless of its origin. It is not a healthy organization when people think good ideas and successful programs only come from senior level leadership. A successful organization will encourage creative thinking from all levels and give credit when a winning idea or solution comes from lower level employees.

4.Educate, train and role play. Teachable moments happen every day in every company. For the business to operate like a team, the members must be informed and trained in best practices. When real life experiences are reflected in training, people will get comfortable and confident with their role in the team.

5.Win and lose as a team. Accomplishments and failures should always be shared as a team. When there is a big account win, the creativity, hard work and commitment of the entire team should be acknowledged. When an account goes bad or experiences a serious problem, the worst situation is to fault any one person. That can be a detriment to the team culture.

6.Encourage social get togethers. One of the best ways for employees to feel attached to a team is to get to know each other on a more personal level. When people are more personally attached to each other, they are more comfortable working together, which helps to build teamwork.

7.Develop team building exercises and programs. Executives routinely have dinners, golf outings, sports events and conferences where relationships are strengthened. However, in some organizations, people at lower levels rarely get to engage in these types of team building activities. Activities don't have to be expensive and they don't have to be too frequent, but they should be made part of the organizational culture. There are also very effective team assessment instruments and workshops to formally analyze team relationships, behavioral traits, and solutions for greater effectiveness.

IT TAKES A VILLAGE

The title of the famous book by Hillary Rodham Clinton has become an expression. The story was based on an old African proverb, "It takes a village to raise a child," which is basically a team concept for society. It takes more than just parents and family, a child will grow and learn from many influences in society – neighbors, schools, churches, etc. A family must reach beyond their inner circle for advice and guidance, and take advantage of all the opportunities that exist in today's world. Some theories in the book are "No family is an island," meaning that the world is too vast to rely only on the nucleus of family to prepare for everything a child is about to encounter. "Every child needs a champion," alluding to positive role models, which can be discovered through all life experiences. "Security takes more than a blanket," conveying that there has to be deep meaning to making a child feel protected, more than just words or material things.

In our society today, not all services are commercial. We have numerous non-profit charity and faith-based organizations that provide essential services around the globe. Much of the work is done by volunteers, who are no less committed to their mission than people doing it for a living. I grew up in two small rural villages. The fire departments were voluntary. Yet when there were fires or accidents, the response was rapid and reliable. Firefighters and EMT's were prepared, equipped and worked with as much precision and dedication as a paid force. They trained and took their responsibilities seriously.

Most of us at different times serve on voluntary teams, whether they be through schools, churches, scouts, little league, home owners associations, charities, or whatever. Very rewarding service, and the better we apply team principles, the more efficient and enjoyable the involvement. These are the organizations that in many cases define our communities. It takes a village.

COLLABORATIVE WORK

The work of every successful team is done through collaboration. Productive collaboration takes the efforts of every team member, the leader cannot do this alone. There are requirements for effective collaboration which I have come across in many articles and teachings, all stated pretty consistently. The U.S. Department of State has even published these steps in their internal policies on conducting effective meetings, identified as the **Seven Norms of Collaborative Work:**

Pausing. Occasional pausing provides for time breaks for everyone to stop and reflect, which has proven to improve critical thinking. Pausing and accepting moments of silence creates a relaxed and purposeful atmosphere. Silence can be an excellent indicator of productive collaboration, because it signals to others that their ideas and comments are worth thinking about. It dignifies their contribution and encourages future participation. Pausing enhances discussion and increases the quality of decision making.

Paraphrasing. To restate or translate into one's own words, to summarize or to provide an example of what has just been said. The paraphrase maintains the intention and the accurate meaning of what has already been said while using different words and phrases. The paraphrase helps members of a team hear and understand each other as they evaluate data and formulate decisions. Paraphrasing is also extremely effective when reducing group tension and individual anger.

Probing. Probing seeks to clarify something which is not yet fully understood. More information may be required or a thought may need to be more fully defined. Clarifying questions can be either specific or open ended, depending upon the circumstances. Gentle probes increase the clarity and precision of a group's thinking and contribute to trust building because they communicate to group members that their ideas are worthy of exploration and consideration.

Putting forward ideas. It takes a degree of self-confidence and courage to put forward an idea, and it is vital that collaborative groups nurture such input. Ideas are the heart of a meaningful discussion. Groups must be comfortable to process information by analyzing, comparing, predicting, applying, or drawing causal relationships.

Paying attention to self and others. Collaborative work is facilitated when each team member is explicitly conscious of self and others. Not only aware of what he or she is saying, but also how it is said and how others are responding to it. We should be curious about other people's impressions and understandings – not judgmental. The more we understand about how someone else processes information, the better we can communicate with them.

Presuming positive presuppositions. This is the assumption that other members of the team are acting from positive and constructive intentions, although we may disagree with their ideas. The assumption of positive intentions permits people to use the role of "devil's advocate," "loyal opposition," or "we agree to disagree." It builds trust, promotes healthy cognitive disagreement, and reduces the likelihood of misunderstanding and conflict.

Pursuing a balance between advocacy and inquiry. Both advocacy and inquiry are necessary components of collaborative work. Highly effective teams are aware of this and attempt to keep them in balance. Inquiry provides for greater understanding. Advocacy leads to decision making. One of the common mistakes that collaborative teams may make is to bring premature closure to problem identification and rush into problem resolution. Maintaining a balance between advocating for a position and inquiring about the positions held by others further enhances the collaborative process.

PATRICK LENCIONI

A renowned management consultant, Patrick Lencioni authored the famous business book, The Five Dysfunctions of a Team. They are worth repeating:

1. Absence of Trust – unwilling to be vulnerable within the group.
2. Fear of Conflict – seeking artificial harmony over constructive passionate debate.
3. Lack of Commitment – feigning buy-in for group decisions creates ambiguity throughout the organization.
4. Avoidance of Accountability – ducking the responsibility to call peers on counterproductive behavior which sets low standards.
5. Inattention to Results – focusing on personal success, status and ego before team success.

"Trust is knowing that when a team member does push you, they're doing it because they care about the team."- Patrick Lencioni

———————————

There are four required elements to achieving team success. They are preparation, focus, passion and trust. To drive a team to success, the dynamic leader must encompass all four.

Chapter 15

Preparation

"Fat, drunk and stupid is no way to go through life son."- Dean Vernon Wormer, Faber College (Animal House)

If you had the desire to run a marathon, would you just show up and run? Of course not, you would train for the event. Would you start training the week before the race? Of course not, you would start a long time ahead. Even people who have never done any long distance running probably understand that the challenge of completing a marathon would take several months of both mental and physical preparation, and involve diet, sleeping habits, sophisticated training with some short and long mileage days, rest days, etc.

When we put our band together, The Happy Javelinas, we practiced for several months, refining the parts for each instrument, changing songs, changing beginnings and endings of songs, changing singing parts, and practicing individually and as a group – all for a one evening performance.

We can understand the importance and necessity of all this preparation for sport or fun activities. Yet in business, some teams form, get together, receive an assignment, and are expected to produce brilliant results with little thought given to proper preparation. There may be a huge dollar amount at stake, but it is assumed that everyone should be able to make this work.

We all have to deal with sales people, and have had experiences with good ones and poor ones. I've had some good relationships with people selling real estate, cars, and of course many selling business services. It is fascinating to observe an expert salesperson at work. They seem confident and at ease talking with the customer. They have their facts, figures, and documents ready to go, and can anticipate and respond to questions or objections that may arise. They have thorough product knowledge, and have the ability to smoothly convince their audience that their product or service will enhance their lives. Customers have an enjoyable experience and feel comfortable in their purchase decision. That type of performance doesn't happen by accident. It is the result of extensive preparation. The salesperson, just like a talented musician or athlete, may make it look easy and effortless, but they have worked hard to learn and practice their skills

In the education field, people are always learning, staying current, and keeping up with technology and techniques. In the highest levels of team sports, they study films of the competition to plan strategy, sometimes hide their injury reports, all to gain a competitive advantage. But back at the office, it's "come on, you guys did this before, you can make it work."

Preparation is obtaining the talent, training for specific roles, forming the team, studying the competition, analyzing the market, following trends, understanding current technology – having the team game ready.

Preparation also takes patience. While there is usually enthusiasm to get started into some form of action, preparation includes the critical planning phase. Depending on the project, the planning and initial stages can be slow moving – obtaining permits, ordering supplies, training, research, hiring people, waiting for customer decisions.

Think of it as refinishing a piece of fine furniture. It may require taking things apart, getting all the needed tools and materials, replacing missing parts, repairing damaged parts, and the painstakingly slow process of hard sanding and fine sanding. Then finally putting on several coats of stain and varnish, and using steel wool after each coat dries to prep for the next layer. To get the immaculate end result, a lot of patience is required for the initial phases and waiting time between each step. Proper preparation may literally be watching paint dry.

ERAS HAVE CHANGED

I am amazed at how preparation has changed. When I graduated from college many years ago, we were told our degree showed that we were an achiever, we had accomplished something very important, and it would open the door to an entry level position. At that point, you had to have the attitude that you were willing to learn, because the degree just gave you the opportunity.

Today we can hire people in many fields right out of college, and they are ready and eager to contribute. They are very well prepared. Their courses of study make them game ready, they have internships where they do real-world applications – not just menial tasks. We recently had an opening in our department for a position that required five to eight years of experience. We received resumes from many applicants, qualified on paper, and many had much more senior experience than we were looking for. We interviewed about a dozen of the 70+ applicants, and did not find any we felt would be a proper fit. I selected a resume of a very recent college graduate who had some good work experience non-related to human resources, and some impressive internship experience in human resources. At the interview she showed confidence and examples of applying the very skills we were seeking. We told her she was not being hired for an entry level job, and we weren't paying her like an entry level job. We were hiring her because we felt she was ready for the job, and she did not disappoint.

We have also seen this in engineering, systems, finance and other disciplines. Students today are getting excellent preparation for the real world. We bring them in and learn from them, in addition to getting help with our personal computer and smart phone questions. They also have the right attitude, business acumen and self-awareness. I am very impressed with today's young people.

I envy the youth of today, with all the opportunities available. However, I also feel fortunate that I grew up in a bygone era of American history. Even for my time, my particular environment was old and outdated. When I described this later to people my own age, they couldn't believe it; because most of my generation grew up in more modern settings. They were even born in hospitals. In the village where I was born, some homes still had outhouses. Although most had indoor bathrooms, some did not. My grandparents did not have an indoor bathroom until they moved when I was in fourth grade. My first three years of school (there was no kindergarten) were in a four room elementary school for eight grades. Four teachers, two grades per room. So when you went from first to second grade, you moved from the left side of the room to the right side of the room. The school did not have indoor toilets, but had a pretty cool multi-stall outhouse, painted yellow. There was a girls and a boys. And they were cleaned every day by the janitor. You don't know what you're missing. No wonder I'm impressed with how students are prepared today.

The village I described was Emerald, Pennsylvania. By fourth grade we had moved a few miles away to Neffs, Pennsylvania. In these wonderful little towns we did not lock the doors of our homes, even when we went away. We didn't take the keys out of the cars or trucks at night, which were in the street or driveway – we didn't have a garage. Today I have a house in a lovely, friendly neighborhood. But we keep our doors locked, even when we are at home, and we have a monitored security system.

Yes, I envy the youth of today, but there is something about my childhood experiences which also gave me preparation for my life and career. I think it has made me impressed with new technologies, more open to change, eager to always continue learning and helping others, and appreciate history and diversity. It definitely molded me for a career in human resources.

WHEN SHOULD PREPARATION BEGIN?

When we form project teams, they sometimes have to go real fast. Ideally, we may desire several months of planning and research, but are often not granted that luxury.

Sports teams usually have a season and schedule. Thus, they have more time to prepare. In fact, there are designated times for off season conditioning and pre-season training camps. Good athletes always try to stay in shape and maintain their condition.

Regardless of your field, there is always constant learning that could be done, so you should always stay current with your occupation, and always in stride with your competition. I remember a football coach who used the expression "If you're not moving forward, you're moving backwards. Because the competition is always improving."

When should preparation begin? Personally, we are in lifelong preparation. As a team, it has to start whenever a team is formed, and whenever there is a change in the team, it has to start over.

I've often heard the expression applied to teams, "A chain is only as strong as its weakest link." This is not usually the case with a team, nor should it be. A superstar can carry a team, and we often have some dynamic team players whom we expect to carry the team. Plus, we have people at different levels – some are there to learn and develop.

"Success is where preparation and opportunity meet."
- Bobby Unser

Remember our communication styles. If a team has dominant, expressive, analytical and amiable members – they can rely on each type for their balancing effect. Together, they will determine their goals, develop their plan, identify their risks, collaborate their ideas, build relationships with customers and stakeholders, and get into action.

Of course, many teams do not have the benefit of this organic balance. Therefore, they must recognize their missing elements and adjust accordingly. Some members must accept roles and responsibilities out of their comfort zone.

In sports, coaches design and implement new game plans on the fly. They may move some people to different positions. They adjust strategy as the game unfolds. Preparation means being ready for adjustments, anticipate that things will go wrong, know what to do when there are injuries.

In a music or theater production, the lead performer may come down with laryngitis. Is the stand-in ready? The show must go on.

Preparation is not easy – but it is where the drive to succeed grows. Athletes may tell you the game is fun, practice is not fun. But the game would be a disaster without practice. Indeed, in most cases, practice should also be fun. Do your part to make it fun.

PREPARATION CHECK LISTS

I have seen checklists to prepare for numerous objectives. How to prepare for a sports contest, a job interview, a sales call, taking an exam, making a speech, doing a solo performance, and many others. No matter what the purpose, they all have things in common, and contain suggestions which are applicable to most any preparation of an individual or team.

Let's start with preparation for a sporting event. Dr. Jack Lesyk of The Ohio Center for Sports Psychology put together a list of nine mental skills for successful athletes.

Attitude: Choose and maintain a positive attitude. The point made is that a person's attitude is a choice, and the choice should be made to focus on the positive. The chosen sport is an opportunity for the athlete to compete against themselves and learn from their successes and failures. Athletes should pursue excellence, not perfection, and realize that they, along with their teammates, coaches, opponents, officials, and support staff, are not perfect. Thus, they should respect their sport, other participants, coaches, officials, and themselves. Lastly, the athletes should maintain balance and perspective between their sport and the rest of their lives.

Motivation. Maintain a high level of self-motivation. Successful athletes are aware of the rewards and benefits that they expect to experience through their sports participation. They are able to persist through difficult tasks and difficult times, even when these rewards and benefits are not immediately forthcoming. Very importantly, athletes must realize that many of the benefits come from their participation, not the outcome.

Goals and commitment. Set high, realistic goals. Athletes should be aware of their current performance levels and be able to develop specific, detailed plans for attaining their goals. They are highly committed to their goals and carrying out the daily demands of their training programs.

People skills. An athlete in any sport must be able to deal effectively with people, and realize that they are part of a larger circle that includes their families, friends, teammates, coaches and fans. They need to communicate and listen. They must develop effective skills for dealing with conflict, difficult opponents, unruly fans, and media personnel when they are negative or oppositional.

Self-talk. It is necessary to maintain self-confidence during difficult times with realistic, positive self-talk to get inside your own head. Use self-talk to regulate thoughts, feelings and behavior during competition. Pump up yourself just like you would talk to your own best friend.

Mental imagery. Athletes must prepare themselves for competition by imagining themselves performing well; visualize the contest. Create and use mental images that are specific and realistic. And use imagery during the event to prepare for action and recover from errors and poor performance.

Dealing effectively with anxiety. An athlete must accept anxiety as part of the sport, and realize that some anxiety can help them perform well. Know how to reduce anxiety when it becomes too strong, without losing intensity.

Dealing effectively with emotions. Managing emotions is a requirement in athletic competition. Accept that strong emotions such as excitement, anger and disappointment are part of the sport experience. Athletes must be able to channel and use these emotions to improve their level of performance.

Concentration. Successful athletes know what they must pay attention to during each game or situation. They must learn how to maintain focus and resist distractions, and be able to regain their focus when concentration is lost during the competition. They must also discipline themselves to concentrate on the now, rather than be distracted by either the past or the anticipated future.

These are all areas for preparation, and can be useful for any type of performance. Now let's look at a preparation checklist for delivering a speech. Again you will see points that could pertain to any type of situational preparation.

Think about the purpose. Is the purpose to inform, to persuade, to entertain, to invoke action? Every speech must have its reason for being.

Analyze the audience. Remember that you are speaking to the audience, so know something about their interests, attitudes, goals, fears. Speak to what they know and care about.

Gather enough material. Start by collecting all your thoughts and notes, then do additional research on the topic. Select only information relevant to the audience and to this particular speech. Your task is to simplify and reinforce.

Clearly convey your purpose. This will become the focus as you put the speech together. Address it in the delivery, perhaps even in the title.

Construct an outline. Lay out your foundation in an outline, and arrange points in the most convincing order.

Prepare visual aids. Your speech may or may not require visual aids. If they are necessary or will enhance your purpose, make sure they are well done and effectively flow with the narrative.

Devise an opening with impact. It may be humorous, surprising, informative, challenging – whatever works for this particular speech. Make your first impression in the introduction, it can assure people that what follows is worth listening to.

Craft your conclusion. End the speech with a strong challenge that tells the audience what you expect them to do with the information just delivered. Conclusions must be memorable.

Write the speech and edit it. Distill your speech down to the essentials, especially if it is technical, to make it easier for the audience to follow. Use short sentences and words, colorful language, sentence fragments, contractions, repetition and questions.

Practice your delivery. In front of a mirror and out loud if possible. Every performance needs practice.

Get your timing down. Part of practicing the delivery is timing the speech. Know how you are going to track your time when giving the speech, be sure you can see a clock or watch.

Make a checklist for the event. Make sure you are prepared ahead of time with incidentals like what you're going to wear; knowing the room or podium set up; knowledge of the visual, sound and lighting operation; bringing copies or handouts; etc.

I have given talks where I went to the location the day before to get a feel for the room or stage, where I was going to stand, and basically walk through the speech. Sometimes everything is provided, and there were times I had to even bring my own extension cord. It can go smooth when there is thorough preparation, but I guarantee when there is not thorough preparation, something is sure to go wrong.

In every kind of performance, anything can go wrong - something was forgotten, a delivery didn't arrive on time, equipment doesn't work, a noisy disturbance occurs in the next room, and numerous other problems. Good preparation will help you anticipate such incidents and how to react to them. Preparation may be preparing for the disaster.

There is no substitute for preparation. Some people pride themselves on their ability to "wing it," and that is a good skill; but thorough forethought and preparation will get you mentally ready to react to the unexpected. The more you rehearse, the better you will be able to think on your feet.

We must prepare ourselves as individuals, and prepare together as a team. And the most important item in all preparation is practice. While few of us have the luxury of committing the 10,000 hours of practice that Malcolm Gladwell states as the requirement for world-class achievement, most of us do not have the goal to be the best in the world at what we do. We just want to be good and keep getting better.

Good Timber
- Douglas Malloch

The tree that never had to fight
For sun and sky and air and light,
But stood out in the open plain
And always got its share of rain,
Never became a forest king
But lived and died a scrubby thing.

The man who never had to toil
To gain and farm his patch of soil,
Who never had to win his share
Of sun and sky and light and air,
Never became a manly man
But lived and died as he began.

Good timber does not grow with ease,
The stronger the wind, the tougher the trees.
The further sky, the greater length,
The more the storm, the more the strength.
By sun and cold, by rain and snow,
In trees and men good timbers grow.

Chapter 16

Focus

"You can observe a lot by just watching."- Yogi Berra

Focus instills determination. The team must focus on the goal and maintain the level of unified determination to achieve victory. Maintaining focus may be one of the most difficult challenges for the team leader. We have seen how the various communication styles of people view basic team procedures with different priorities. Yet a successful team is required to maintain a unified focus on the mission and vision of the team, as well as the organization.

Focus on the purpose, and on the positive. Legendary football coach, now famous restaurateur, Don Shula, has a 24-hour rule to keep people looking forward, and focus on the purpose while staying positive. He states that the focus must be on the next challenge. Thus, he allows a maximum of 24 hours to celebrate a victory or brood over a defeat. Then put it behind and concentrate your energy on the next opponent. He had great success with this rule in sports, now applies it to his business ventures.

The examples throughout this book of successful business and sports leaders illustrates their special talent for unifying a group of people into a team with a common purpose. They made the team believe in themselves and become devoted to team success. Together, they developed trust, and shared a team focus.

"I don't focus on what I'm up against. I focus on my goals and I try to ignore the rest."- Venus Williams

The enemy of focus is distractions. As Venus Williams states, focus on goals and try to ignore the rest. But ignoring the rest is not easy. Do you think athletes really ignore the boo's? Why is trash talking so effective? Why does negative campaigning work? Everyone in any type of competition tries to play mind games with their opponent to create a distraction that will break their focus. The more focused we are, the more successful we can be at whatever we do. Conversely, the more distracted, the less well we can accomplish our objective. Distractions are often referred to as a wandering mind.

"You can't depend on your eyes when your imagination is out of focus."- Mark Twain

In today's world we are surrounded by attention busters. We're all carrying a phone. At any time we may get a call, message or email. Whether business related or personal, it creates a distraction from what we were doing, and on where our attention had been focused.

We all fall into the wandering mind syndrome at times – daydreaming, we're on auto-pilot. We may be concentrating on another problem or subject, reliving a funny incident, doing creative thinking, or just playing a song in our head. Therefore, when running a team meeting, we must make special effort to keep the audience focused on the job at hand.

People are not as automatically enthusiastic about the message like you are. So your presentation has to be planned accordingly. Plan ahead to be inspiring. To do this you have to know your team, or your audience. What will excite them, what will discourage them?

HOW WAS YOUR WEEK?

I sat next to a guy on a plane and we were talking about this very thing – maintaining focus. He told me about the practice he uses with this team. I found it to be fascinating, and want to share it. At the end of each week he has every one of his direct reports send him a short note to tell him how their week was. He wants them to spend no more than 15 minutes doing this, and he generally spends less than five minutes reading each one. The note is titled "How Was Your Week?"

He is amazed at how much information he learns about his people, the customers, service standards, production issues, delivery problems, product questions, and such. People share their feelings and explain concerns. They also report team news, such as positive comments or special coworker contributions. They make recommendations for changes. They relay client comments, both good and bad. He has found that it is easier for people to express these things in writing, where they can think, edit, and put thoughts together – before hitting send. Face to face, they would not enunciate these things as well, or perhaps not bring them up at all. There is much less pressure on the people to write and email a note than verbally speaking. The company has uncovered and discussed many problems they were not aware they even had. He started this practice with his direct reports, now it is used throughout his company.

"100% of the shots you don't take, don't go in."- Wayne Gretzky

During an interview Wayne Gretzky was asked what he focuses on when on the ice. He said, "Our job is to put the puck in the net." Simply put, that is the purpose. To do this, he said he doesn't go to where the puck is, he goes to where the puck is going to be. His famous quote above has been applied to many aspects of business – 100% of the shots you don't take, don't go in. Take the shot. Don't always wait for the perfect moment, the perfect situation – take the shot, propose your idea, and a lot of good things can happen.

Wayne Gretzky, nicknamed "The Great One," set so many scoring records in hockey, far too many to list in this book. When he retired as an active player he held 61 National Hockey League records. He was certainly focused on putting the puck in the net. Just as impressive were the careers of a number of other hockey scoring greats, who had the opportunity to play on his teams. Jari Kurri, Mark Messier, Esa Tikkanen, Bernie Nicholls, Tony Granato, Thomas Sandstrom, Luc Robitaille, among others, had their most proficient seasons when they were on the ice with Wayne Gretzky as a teammate. He maintained his own focus, and inspired his team. He made his teammates better, and brought out the best in them. They would put themselves in a position to score, and he would pass them the puck. He served as Captain of four different NHL teams, and always had an ability to inspire others and maintain a team focus.

ABRAHAM LINCOLN

A challenge for both an individual and a team is keeping your focus despite failure. Your goal and purpose must be very strong, and not waver in times of defeat. Discouragement is another form of distraction, which is the enemy of focus.

We can take a lesson from Abe Lincoln, one of our country's most important historical figures, one of our greatest Presidents, who preserved the Union through the Civil War. If you think he was deterred by defeat, look at his career record:

- Failed in business at age 21.
- Defeated in a state of Illinois legislative race at age 24.
- Overcame death of his sweetheart at age 26.
- Had a nervous breakdown at age 27.
- Lost a US congressional race at age 34.
- Lost a US congressional race at age 36.
- Elected to US House of Representatives at age 38, served 2 years.
- Lost a US senatorial race at age 45.
- Failed in an effort to become Vice President at age 47.
- Elected President of the United States at age 52.

In the controversial presidential general election of 1860 there were four candidates. Lincoln won by a narrow margin in the North, and lost every Southern state. By the time he was inaugurated, seven Southern states had seceded. He had to sneak into Washington in disguise to avoid a planned assassination attempt aboard the train he was reported to be on. With all that in his background, he had a focus to unite the country.

TEAM FOCUS

Building and maintaining focus as a team is the ultimate goal. When a team can get to a high energy level as a unit, and that dedication is sustained, then the team is achieving excellence. What are things the leader can do to maintain that level of achievement?

Focus on the challenge. The common driver for the team is the challenge. Sports teams often have slogans on the board in the locker room, or a sign above the exit to the field, where everyone on the team constantly sees this reminder of their challenge.

Deliver the message. A good coach is a good communicator. Each has their individual style. Use your own, don't try to be someone else. There are locker room motivational talks which have become legendary. Some leaders have a knack for being inspirational.

When making a presentation to the team, don't just present – build, and involve team members in the development. A power point presentation is not as good as a whiteboard, where you can involve people and capture their input. A study at Stanford University School of Business found that participants were more engaged by a whiteboard presentation and retained more of the information later than all other common presentation methods.

Keep the team informed on everything that is happening and affecting progress, such as customer feedback, delays, changing schedule, and such. Teams do not operate on auto pilot. They need to be informed with frequent communications.

Team relationship. Team bonding does not just happen by nature. It must be formed and constantly reinforced. A leader must look for problems or dysfunctions, because breakdowns can happen at any time. Many team relationships are fragile, especially if there is an issue between two principal members. In the successful teams, the relationships are solid. A leader should be as friendly as possible with team members, and encourage them to bond. When this occurs, the trust level is increased.

This is especially important when deadlines get close and the stress level increases. It eventually leads to complete reliance on trust of each team member to deliver their respective work. We want the team to feel safe and secure with the ability to take measured risks as we move forward. This is done through trust among team members, as well as trust in the leader.

Recognize team accomplishments. Everyone hears the messages of problems and negatives on the project, so it is very important to celebrate the successes along the way. Knowing that things done well have been noticed and appreciated will encourage the team to stay focused and continue to produce at a higher standard. Rewards and recognition can be big or small, monetary or non-monetary, but they all matter deeply and are highly appreciated. Nothing builds team pride more than honest team recognition.

Keep the positive attitude. It takes a strong source of positive energy to influence the attitude of the entire team. Effective team leaders always keep a positive attitude. They need to maintain the positive attitude to motivate the rest of the team to stay confident. The upbeat, energetic, and confident attitude of the leader will create a pleasant and comfortable environment for the team to function.

Know the process, see the results, know why their work is important. Through effective communication, everyone should be aware of the steps, timelines and assignments for critical parts of the project – and their personal important part of the project. Some group work is long term and enduring, such as construction. People can look at what they helped to build for years and always feel that pride. Whereas some group work is short term, completed quickly, then the team begins a new one. An example of this is the hospitality industry. It can take many people and many specialists to pull off an event, such as a large business conference, wedding, graduation ceremony, Presidential inauguration. Then it ends, people clean up, and we regroup the teams for the next program. Another type is where some people are only a small part of the process, with little or no involvement in the finished product. An example of this is manufacturing. Some people make their living for many years in one step of the assembly line, where they only see and do their stage of the final product.

I did human resources work in each of these industries – construction, hospitality and manufacturing. I saw workers of all levels having pride in their work, the products or services, and the company. They were made to feel that their contribution was crucial to the overall successful customer experience, which it was. Each function takes focus, motivation and pride in their contribution.

It's like the fable of the rock miners, where two workers were extracting rocks out of a mountain. The first one was asked what he was doing, and he replied that he is mining rocks, and we have to fill that wagon with rocks every day. It's hard work but it's a good job.

The second miner was asked what he was doing, and he replied that he was part of a team that is building a new cathedral. My job is the first stage, so I must meet production and select good quality rocks because other people down the line, like the stone masons, are depending on me.

People are more likely to stay focused on their tasks and find motivation in their team when they know that their results matter and are appreciated.

Engagement. Everyone needs to be given a chance to talk and participate in decisions. The best teams are in frequent communications, outside of the formal meetings. A leader must encourage all members to engage and share their opinions. This means the leader must sometimes be skilled at trying to control those who are outspoken or attempting to take over. Someone may be so emotionally charged over a given topic or project, that they will try to shut off all alternative opinions. A good team knows that flexibility is required for success – they must be open to change and new ideas, and every team member must feel their views will be taken into consideration.

FOCUS ON CONTINUOUS IMPROVEMENT

We want to develop a learning culture in our organizations. That should include everyone, from presidents to interns. When should people stop participating in development programs? When they know it all. And although I've never met anyone who is an expert at everything, I have known many people, particularly in senior management, who would not participate in any seminar or learning program. They felt it was beneath them, insulting to their level; yet in some cases they had not attended such a program in one or two decades. No wonder they are resistant to change. In those cases, we had to focus on everyone else. We would hear a consistent message – this is great information, but the senior leaders should also get this training. They are the ones who need it. Oh, the frustrations.

There are a number of continuous improvement models which are very good for team production and focus. Theories like Lean, Kaizen and Six Sigma are popular and produce remarkable results for many companies, and unify the participating teams. Is continuous improvement a relatively new concept? Hardly. Some may say they remember the Total Quality Management push in the 80's, leading to the Malcolm Baldridge National Quality Award. Other business historians say they heard it grew out of the movements after World War II, when American industrialists were helping to rebuild the manufacturing and infrastructure in Japan. Through this movement people like Edwards Deming, Armand Feigenbaum, Joseph Juran, Homer Sarasohn and others pioneered the theories of quality management, data systems control, and employee participation. But the concept goes back way further.

"He who stops being better stops being good." - Oliver Cromwell

Oliver Cromwell was an English military and political leader in the 1600's. He was a prominent figure during the English Civil War who helped to remove King Charles I from power in 1649. He was later appointed to the position of Lord Protector of the Commonwealth of England, Scotland and Ireland. How's that for a title. He established a concept called the New Model Army, where for the first time people were recruited, and officers selected, on merit, not social class. Even that long ago, and in such a class society as old England, Oliver Cromwell saw the merits in people from all backgrounds, encouraged continuous improvement and self-worth, and tried to implement these changes in the military and also in government.

FOCUS ON THE PURPOSE

To unite a team effort there must be an understanding shared by all, of the team purpose. All members should know their role and purpose, as well as the team's role and purpose. I will illustrate by example how we have done this in our Human Resources Department. It is something I recommend for all departments or teams, before you proceed any further. It should be step one – develop the function chart, to answer the question "what is our purpose"? In our case we identified three areas – Organizational Direction, Employee Excellence, and HR Programs. These were then sub-divided into the various elements of each for which we intended to develop programs and initiatives, and assign those responsibilities to designated people.

The function chart should be developed before the organization chart, where names and titles are inserted. Design the people structure and assignments around the purpose. Otherwise, you have people with titles, and allow things to fall into their respective place, perhaps without the passion, preparation or direction required taken into consideration.

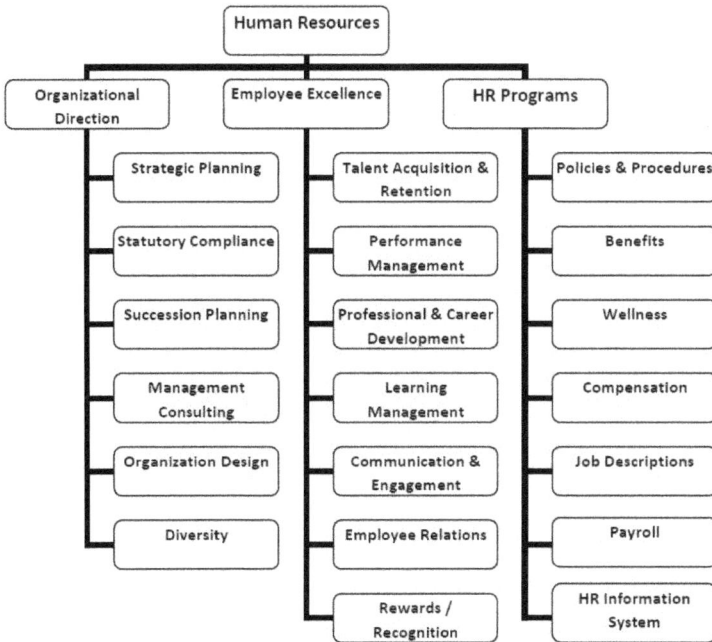

```
                          Human Resources
                 |               |                 |
    Organizational       Employee Excellence      HR Programs
      Direction
          |                      |                     |
   Strategic Planning    Talent Acquisition &    Policies & Procedures
                              Retention
          |                      |                     |
  Statutory Compliance      Performance               Benefits
                            Management
          |                      |                     |
  Succession Planning    Professional & Career       Wellness
                            Development
          |                      |                     |
     Management              Learning               Compensation
     Consulting            Management
          |                      |                     |
 Organization Design     Communication &         Job Descriptions
                            Engagement
          |                      |                     |
      Diversity           Employee Relations         Payroll
                               |                     |
                            Rewards /             HR Information
                           Recognition              System
```

In summary, focus must be maintained by every member of the team, and it must be a common focus – on the tasks, the purpose, the future, the possibilities, the big picture, the vision, and the team as a whole.

Perhaps the best quote on focus, at least the funniest, was from the movie Caddyshack, when Ty Webb was giving instructions to Danny Noonan on how to focus on his golf shot:

"There's a force in the universe that makes things happen. All you have to do is get in touch with it. Stop thinking, let things happen, and be the ball. Be the ball, Danny. Be the ball."

Chapter 17

Passion

"Passion isn't something that lives way up in the sky, in abstract dreams and hopes. It lives at ground level, in the specific details of what you're actually doing every day." - Marcus Buckingham

We all have passions. It might be for our favorite sports teams, our heroes, our college, our favorite activities, our favorite charity, or our favorite vacation spots. We want people to know about these passions – they see our tee shirts; pictures, trinkets and coffee mugs in our home and office. Our passions give us a great feeling, a purpose to get excited about, and we love talking about them.

We can get into friendly arguments, although sometimes intense, with people who don't share our passions – especially if they have an opposing one. This usually doesn't affect the spirit of the team, as long as we are talking about things like sports, schools, vacations, cars (when I was young, most everyone was on one side or the other of the Ford vs. Chevy argument). In fact, good-natured differences can make a team more fun and interesting.

But think how feelings can escalate when the subject is politics, or political issues like abortion or gun control. Now think how much more intense it sometimes gets in the workplace. Disagreements over the value or ethics of a particular employee, feelings towards a certain customer, concerns over a potential acquisition or partnership, a product specification, a marketing plan.

Diversity is a good thing for a team in many ways, but can be a problem when there is a conflict of passions. People must be mature enough to enjoy the rivalries, accept the differences of opinions, and not let them affect the unity of the work team.

"Just one word. Are you listening? Plastics."
- Mr. McGuire's career advice to Benjamin in The Graduate

We probably all have known someone who started college and picked a major that was recommended by a parent, uncle, teacher, or boss at their summer job. They may have used rationale like, "those jobs are always in demand; that field really pays well; you can write your own ticket; you'll always have a job."

In some cases it was great advice. Many times, however, the student either changes their major, drops out, or graduates – then goes into a different line of work, either right away or within a few years.

The problem – the student did not have a passion for that particular field of study. You will be successful in what you have a passion for, and miserable in what you do not.

Many people just naturally go into the family business because they are expected to. Some have a passion for the business. After all, they were raised in it. But some do not, and it is wrong for them to follow, and wrong for their family to force it. This can also be the case with the traditional occupation in the family. Many family members were all in the military, or all in the medical field, or all engineers, or all teachers – so they expect the child to follow suit. This can result in a terrible injustice to that child's happiness and potential for success.

Some people wonder if passion is something we are born with, or are passions developed. It seems like there is some of both. While we may not be born with passions, some are formed early due to the environments just mentioned. We are greatly influenced by our families. When you grow up in a family of New York Yankee fans, you are likely to become a New York Yankee fan yourself.

But most passions are formed as we go through life and are influenced by our own environments and experiences. We may take a new job, and soon have passions for a new company, new industry, and new occupation.

Thus, it is the role of the dynamic team leader to demonstrate a passion for the team, their function, and the organization. A leader will inspire passion in the individual members, harness it, develop team passion, and blend it to create team energy.

Generating passion and keeping team members passionate is a major task for the leader. At the start of a project, commitment to the overall goals and purpose can be easy for the team. However, as the project progresses, the group may occasionally need to refocus and re-energize. The passions can fade, and it is everyone's responsibility to have this awareness and right the ship. This is especially a key role of the leader, the team captain, or the assigned champion of a particular project.

Communications are vital to keep everyone involved, informed and enthusiastic. Nothing will destroy team passion and commitment quicker than a breakdown in sharing information.

Purpose and appreciation must be reinforced. Bring back the excitement that was generated when the program was announced. Have frequent meetings, and reaffirm the commitment to the importance of the project. Share the recognition, appreciation, as well as the problems.

Don't leave anyone out, this is a team dynamic. Everyone should be reminded of the importance of their role, even if it is just to observe and learn. The leader should make themselves available to all team members.

The leader must also stay close to the team members, and watch for formation of cliques and silos. Guide the team through changes. As growth occurs, and team members change or restructure, passion may be lost. Organic growth can bring cultural changes, even more so with growth through merges and acquisitions. Layoffs and downsizing are the ultimate destroyer of passion.

To keep moving forward, there must be a shared sense of purpose and identity. Sometimes people see change as a sign of progress, which will bring new growth opportunities.

Here comes a potential conflict. People at the top, especially founders and long-term senior management, can be reluctant to change a company's purpose and identity, usually stated very carefully in the company's mission statement. However, the mission statement should be reviewed, challenged, and revised if necessary, on a routine basis as a sign of flexibility and progress. Especially after market changes or new lines of business are implemented.

Look at advertising campaigns. Television commercials for fast food, soft drinks, insurance, cars and trucks, etc. The basic product may stay the same, but small changes in packaging, style, flavor, size or whatever, may make it feel like something different and exciting. It's always new and improved. Marketing will come up with new slogans, jingles, purposes, lifestyles – this is the all new campaign that will change the world.

The mission may stay the same – make a good product, sell it at a fair price, meet customers' needs. But the internal passion of the workforce can be renewed motivation for this new product launch and marketing campaign.

I hear too many leaders asking how to keep workers passionate on their task. I sometimes say don't – let them find passion in the big picture, reinforce the importance of their function, and its role to overall company success. Every job is important or we wouldn't have it. Promote the excitement of the overall objectives, and welcome their questions and suggestions. Provide the opportunity for everyone to feel engaged. Hold routine town hall meetings so everyone hears the message. Trust me, the "trickle down" form of communication does not work. We want everyone "in the zone" with the intensity to do their part for team success. That is the passion that leadership must instill, and nothing does it better than sharing and inclusion, transparency and openness, trust and compassion.

We talked about family businesses and family occupations. There are family cultures formulated around beliefs and passions. Some family cultures can get disrupted, and various members may be unable to adapt or accept the differences. Such things like change of family religion to another faith or to no religion, choice of a school or career, choice of a mate, different lifestyle or sexual orientation. Any of these can have a profound effect on family culture. Likewise, there are passions held for business culture; and some leaders have difficulty dealing with the change. There is a book titled Change or Die, using illustrations where people will choose to die, rather than change. From patients suffering with heart disease, to repeat offenders in the criminal justice system, to companies using unsuccessful business practices. One example is smoking – even in some cases where a patient was told, actually we have all been told – that you either stop smoking or it will cause you to die. Those who continue to smoke have chosen the die option over the quit option, usually because the process of change was just too difficult. In business, we frequently encounter the change or die option (perhaps better understood as the change or fail option, or the change or lose money option). When change in business has such a huge potential downside, and passion is held so strongly that it may be left to fail, the leader and the team must join together and change the outdated mode of thinking.

DISCOVER YOUR PASSIONS

"There is no passion to be found playing small – in settling for a life that is less than the one you are capable of living."- Nelson Mandela

To many people, passion isn't something that has to be discovered, they have plenty of them. But to others, they may feel that there is nothing that really gets them excited about life. Indeed, they envy the people they see getting so excited about things – they wish they could find that passion in something.

Passion can be generated from several sources. One is pleasure – what things give you the personal enjoyment that makes you want to do them again and again? It could be something as simple as listening to music. A certain type of music, a few specific groups or singers. Let yourself enjoy it, set aside priority time to listen to it. It will build, and open your mind to other related pleasures. Soon you'll be going to concerts.

Another source is your purpose, which you may not have yet discovered. What do you want to be? What are your beliefs? You may have tried any number of occupations, hobbies, and volunteer work trying to find where you belong. You're likely trying too hard to find your purpose, and not taking the time to enjoy the little things along the way. Rather than finding your purpose in what you have done; first follow your beliefs and interests, and let the activities fall in place.

A third source to develop passion is timing. You may love a great vacation spot, but only go there every few years. It may be participating in an event, but that is only once a year. You have the control. Identify the things you really enjoy in these ventures, then find other outlets where you can do them much more frequently. If you can't get to Paris, bring Paris to you – find alternatives for the meantime.

In time, your passions will capture you, and drive you to new goals. When people really enjoy something, they find it easier to do. If you have enjoyment for a certain topic, you will learn it easier. Students who follow their passion when selecting their course of study, will do better and enjoy it more.

Passion also sparks creativity. Since you think about it more, and want to talk about it more, creative thinking will be generated. Thus, the people who have passion for their job or the type of work will make the best employees. When you have this passion, you feel like you would do it for free. When I was young and worked as a ski instructor, I couldn't believe I was actually getting paid to do it. I loved it and would definitely have done it for free. Of course, the amount of money I made was pretty close to doing it for free.

We all have some dreams and fantasies. And life is full of obligations and commitments that we must give first priority. That's just the way it is. We certainly find fulfillment in our families, our homes, and our jobs. But envision yourself 25 years from now, and think if there is anything you would regret not having tried. We can list many things that we have never done, and never will do. I'll never walk on the Great Wall of China, or climb Mount Everest. But I don't want to, and I'm satisfied seeing it on television. But if there are one or two compelling desires that you keep putting off, yet the interest remains – that is the passion calling. Passion also generates your excitement and builds your confidence. Just do it.

PASSION FOR YOUR WORK

Surveys have consistently shown that over 50% of people are unhappy in their jobs. They keep their job because it is a means to pay their bills. They could describe their dream job, but they can't get one. Some of them look for that job, while many have given up trying. I have worked with numerous people in this dilemma who question if they should start their own business. Some do, some don't want to, some can't.

Starting your own business can be a wonderful experience, and there are thousands of success stories. If you talk to someone who is happy in this role, they do not speak about their income, but about their freedom, flexibility, control, and passion. That is the element for success in starting a business – following your passion. The wrong reason is opening a business out of frustration in not finding employment. People who do this usually look into a franchise opportunity, sometimes in a field they know nothing about. They are doomed for frustration and failure.

So our goal is to find the job or start the business that will follow our passion. Starting a business is often referred to as buying yourself a job. There's nothing wrong with that, as long as it will make you happy. One way or another, we all want to find our dream job. For many people just being an entrepreneur is their passion, and they may change businesses or keep adding new ventures.

We all talk about our passions, but few of us apply it to our job – some don't even think their work should be their source of fun or passion fulfillment. We've all seen friends who are generally happy people, but they hate their job. What a sad way to spend one-third of the hours in a workweek. They might tell you their true passion is fishing, or playing golf, or working with their show horses – but they still have to work.

I say it is great to enjoy your hobbies and outside interests, and it makes for valuable family time. But also make a conscious effort to find passion in your day job. You can do both.

If you hate your job, get a different one. If you hate the whole idea of working, and you are not independently wealthy, you have a problem. There is no reason you cannot find enjoyment in your work. The workplace is where most people meet new friends. Our work enables innovation and creativity – seriously, no matter what the job. As long as we keep a positive attitude towards our work, it intensifies our energy and focus. It also provides an opportunity to learn, grow and pursue excellence.

———————————

I read a question in a newspaper that a person asked about finding a job with a good boss. He explained that he had worked at four places and had four crazy bosses. His question was what could he do at an interview to make sure he got someone he would enjoy working with. The advice columnist responded that the common denominator in the four cases was him. He should focus on his own attitude, rather than assuming through coincidence he happened to find four crazy bosses.

Anne Bechard conducted interviews and wrote an article about the key things people who love their jobs do differently. She centered on five elements that made a difference. These are five realizations that anyone can do with the proper mindset:

They follow their passion. People who love their jobs also do what they love at home, no matter what they do at work. They follow their passion right now, any way they can. They don't wait until they can do it full-time. They realize that their job doesn't have to be their total passion, and sometimes it works out better to keep their hobbies completely separate. They don't resent their job for getting in the way of doing the things they love. They appreciate their job for the security it affords them to pursue their other interests.

They look for happy people. People who are happy with their lives and enjoy working every day hang around other people who are happy too. They don't let the people who thrive on gossip and resist new ideas drag them down. Instead, they practice constructive habits with others. They look for positive people who build up the workplace rather than tearing it down with negativity.

They start their day the way they want to finish it. People who are happy at work deliberately set the tone for the entire day. From the time they get up, they make an effort to create a calm, positive mindset.

They do not fall victim to the drama queens. They enjoy being at work because they practice how to think clearly, lose the bad attitude, and stay motivated through the day.

They don't expect their job to make them happy. They create their own fulfillment and feel useful both in and out of the workplace. People who love their jobs are already satisfied. They don't need their job to make them a satisfied person.

They prefer excellence over perfection. People who love their job always do their best. Whether at home or work, they pursue excellence in whatever they undertake. They don't beat themselves up if things don't go just as planned. They realize that no one achieves perfection all the time. They can always take pride in a job well done, because their outcomes meet their standard of excellence.

So what can you do if you're still not convinced that you can find peace and enjoyment in your job? First, analyze the root of the problem. This may take someone to help you analyze the situation. You are no longer passionate about your work, so go back and determine when and how things went wrong. Once you have determined that, you can start making changes to yourself and your work environment to improve the situation. The necessary conversations and changes may not come easy, but give it your most sincere effort.

Next, you may have to find your new meaning. The business, people, and your own values may have changed significantly over the years, and you may not want to cope with the way things have developed. Wrestle with your own mind and determine what you want to do going forward. This is a long-term, big picture decision. Don't make major changes for a short-term cure.

Challenge yourself. Doing work at which you lost your passion will lead to stress, and that will affect your whole being. Find the balance for all of your interests. Look for ways to make improvements for you and for the company.

Draw strength from others. Make an extra effort to talk with people and make new friends. Network with people in the company or even the industry, which can help you regain your productivity and enthusiasm. Get involved in the community and other new interests. Go out of your way to help others. Being a mentor to someone new is a great way to restore the passion for what you do.

When have you felt the most joy at work? What gives you energy and makes you feel excited and appreciated? You can get to that point again.

WARREN BUFFET

Now here is someone who is passionate about his work. First of all, he is still working years after he could have retired. Warren Buffet is among the world's wealthiest people, and is Chairman/CEO of Berkshire Hathaway.

Buffet is famous for being a business leader, investor and philanthropist. He has pledged to give away 99 percent of his fortune to philanthropic causes, primarily through the Gates Foundation.

He still lives in the same house he purchased in 1958 for $31,500. It is a nice house, I have seen a picture of it. But come on, if I had his money I would live in a home that looked like Buckingham Palace. He also drives his own car. His children all went to public school – on the bus!

Here is a man with passion who is doing it for love, not for money. A born entrepreneur, Warren Buffet filed his first income tax return at age 14, because he had so many means of income going. He worked in his grandfather's grocery store, delivered newspapers, detailed cars, sold golf balls and stamps. He also owned several pinball machines with a buddy which they had in local barber shops. This was all while still in high school. Before he graduated from high school, he was buying stock, invested in a business with his father, and purchased a farm worked by a tenant farmer. To this day, when Warren Buffet invests in businesses, he does research to see if management is candid and honest with shareholders. He looks into the values of the enterprise and the values of its leadership. He lives by his values in business, in charity, and with his family. He is truly a man driven by passion.

TEAM PASSION

Some of the most passionate teams earning a livelihood can be found in police, firefighters, the military, and similar public defenders. It's easy to understand why – they train together, they live together, they share personal stories and commitment. They also depend on each other for their life, and the lives of others. These are passion-driven teams.

As leaders, we must try to instill that kind of team passion and camaraderie in all of our work teams. This becomes more possible when, like the types of teams referred to above, we can blend personal values and goals with the team operating principles and objectives. The team leader must lead by example, be a positive role model, address and solve conflicts, and encourage celebrations. The leader is the driver of team synergy, which is done by getting everyone emotionally connected. It is a big challenge, and can be done through the following steps:

Trust your team. Trust goes both ways, you must earn their trust in you, and you must trust them until they betray their commitment. Recognize employees who help others and contribute to the company. Don't confine people to their job descriptions, open up their empowerment and let the group soar.

Communicate the purpose. Align the team's work objectives with corporate objectives. This common purpose will drive commitment. Even a "Team of Rivals" will unite and be driven for a common purpose. Plus, people will feel more comfortable with change when they fully understand the vision. Share the vision and high level decisions with the team so they feel respect and inclusion.

Team precision, direction and discipline. A team must work together with precision like a drill team, and appear united in the eyes of the customer. This is a sign of good coaching and leadership, and is started with a thorough explanation of the rules, boundaries and direction. By discipline we mean the professional control to not go outside of the boundaries or parameters where doing so would jeopardize the mission. Now here are some contradictions which the dynamic leader must keep in balance. We want everyone to know the rules and show discipline; but we want to sometimes break the rules to foster creativity. We want to empower employees to feel liberated and autonomous; but as a team we want to share and develop joint resolutions.

Be a good listener. A good leader is a good listener – hear the input from everyone on the team. Their thoughts and opinions may change just like yours do, so listening is an ongoing process. Watch for expressions and body language, they may not speak their opinions but they may show them. Include people in meetings and discussions to gain their perspective, they will be motivated and educated by their involvement.

Provide meaningful opportunities. People want to be challenged, and given the opportunity to apply their talent to meaningful work. This means the leader must assess the capabilities of the team members and make assignments accordingly. Partner people up to both utilize their strengths, and also provide them with exposures to learn. Ensure that people are in roles that can make the best application of their skills. Successful teams don't see problems, they see opportunities.

Share successes and failures. A team is all in, together. So when there is success, it should be recognized and celebrated. Not everything requires a brass band – just acknowledgement with proper thanks, coffee and cake, group lunch, whatever. Everyone should share in the success, and the leader should be the biggest cheerleader. Likewise, when things go wrong, be open and hold the team accountable. The team is a responsible unit, and there will be mistakes. Use them as a learning experience.

Passion means wanting something more than anything else. It may stem from the love of the game, the team, the profession, the company, the industry. With passion for excellence, you bring out the best in yourself, your team, and even your opponent.

The following poem always seems to inspire passion.

Don't Quit
- Author unknown

When things go wrong, as they sometimes will,
When the road you're trudging seems all uphill,
When funds are low and the debts are high,
And you want to smile but you have to sigh,
When care is pressing you down a bit,
Rest if you must, but don't you quit.

Life is queer with its twists and turns,
As every one of us sometimes learns,
And many a failure turns about,
When we might have won if we'd stuck it out.
Don't give up though the pace seems slow,
You might succeed with another blow.

Often the goal is nearer than
It seems to a faint and faltering man;
Often the struggler has given up
When he might have captured the victor's cup.
And he learned too late, when the night slipped down,
How close he was to the golden crown.

Success is failure turned inside out,
The silver tint of the clouds of doubt.
And you never can tell how close you are,
It may be near when it seems so far.
So stick to the fight when you're hardest hit,
It's when things seem worst that you must not quit.

Chapter 18

Trust

"You may be deceived if you trust too much, but you will live in torment if you don't trust enough." - Frank Crane

What drives an individual is faith; what drives a team is trust (Psychology 101). Trust is an essential component of a successful team. Teams with participants who trust each other's decisions and actions can work faster to accomplish goals, whereas teams whose members do not trust each other will waste time discussing next steps and micromanaging each other's ideas. Team members who trust each other have nothing to fear from healthy conflict and challenge, which reduces the likelihood that people will agree to an idea just because they are afraid of the consequences if they disagree. It takes time to build trust in a team, so what may start as a weakness can become a strength over time.

Everyone wants to feel they can be trusted, but not everyone conducts themselves in a way to earn trust from others. People with high responsiveness (expressives and amiables), build relationships on trust and generally are willing to trust others. People with lower responsiveness (dominants and analyticals), are more guarded with their emotions, take a cautious approach before trusting others, and deal more with facts and tasks than relationships.

"Getting good players is easy. Getting them to play together is the hard part."- Casey Stengel

Building a team should be synonymous with building trust. There is a long-running debate about giving trophies to every kid who participates in youth sports versus only giving them to the winners. On one side of the debate are people who think it teaches the wrong message to give everyone a trophy. Children should be taught at an early age that only the winners get rewarded. They won't develop the drive to excel if a trophy is given to the losing team. Even in school, you don't get rewarded for just showing up, you have to earn your grades.

Well, I'm on the other side of that argument. I don't see any harm in every kid receiving a trophy or ribbon for participating. After all, we're talking here about youth sports programs, kids in grade school ages. It's fine to give the winning team a different color award – they won the gold. But it is not going to tarnish any child later in life because they got a little plastic trophy that they and their parents were proud of to put on their shelf. They were given that recognition because they participated, stayed with the program, gave their best effort – oh yes, and were part of a team. The team was given their trophies together.

Even on the team that finished in first place, won the championship, they all got the same trophy. The kids who were mostly on the bench and played sparingly, felt as much a part of the team as the ones who were the stars. They all had fun, camaraderie, and sportsmanship.

"When a team outgrows individual performance and learns team confidence, excellence becomes a reality."- Joe Paterno

Joe Paterno spent his whole life building teams, with some new members replacing departing members every year. Like Casey Stengel, he got good athletes, but molding them into a successful team was the hard part. Penn State is famous for plain uniforms with no name on the back of the jersey. It is their way of saying they are all for the team, not for individual recognition.

"It is amazing how much you can accomplish when it doesn't matter who gets the credit."- Harry S. Truman

The quote by Harry Truman shows the same logic applies to teams outside of sports. When members truly care about the mission, and their purpose is achieving that goal – they accomplish their success through team effort because it works the best. And the more they trust each other, they can depend on each other, and their chances of success will increase.

Respect and trust are often used together. They are two different things, and it is possible to have either one without the other. You can respect someone's ability, but do not trust that they will be there for you. Conversely, you can trust someone's dedication and loyalty, but do not respect their knowledge or experience on a given topic to handle it properly. When you have both, the bond is dynamic. That is another factor which the coach or leader should have as a priority – to establish respect and trust among all members.

We have discussed the expression that a chain is only as strong as its weakest link. In certain circumstances that can be true. However, the responsibility of both the leader and all team members is to strengthen the weakest link. Supporting one another is true team commitment.

So how does a successful leader build rapport among all team members? It is not always easy, there are some people who are difficult to work with and are not the team-bonding type. The leader must be persistent and work with the indifferent person. Maybe it takes just being an understanding friend to bring them around. Maybe it takes some assessments and training. Maybe they are not worth the high maintenance and should be moved out. We cannot let one bad apple destroy the team, which is not fair to everyone else.

An effective leader uses consensus building methods to create harmony in the team. He or she must know how to use the strongest people to bring out the engagement in others. Having everyone share their opinions and feelings towards a common purpose is a great step to building the respect and trust among the team. Part of consensus building is conflict avoidance or resolution. Healthy disagreements are necessary, and everyone should feel empowered to make recommendations. The leader should have the ability to clarify the problems and suggestions expressed, and engage others in finding the resolution.

The effective leader also leads by example, and shows respect and trust to the team. This means having open and transparent communications. Some things cannot be shared, but share what you can. Nothing kills trust of the leader more than constant secrecy. People who think information is power, so if I hold all the information I hold all the power, make terrible managers.

Get to know every member of the team personally. Add some social activities to the work routine, so everyone gets to know one another a little more as people, not just as a coworker. This not only builds trust, but also helps to stop the formation of cliques within the group.

THE TRUST EQUATION

Dr. Ricardo Azziz wrote about critical elements for building a high performing team which he called the Trust Equation. Trust is what fosters the building of families, communities and nations; as well as what allows us to engage in commerce, in friendships and relationships. Trust gives us the ability to predict positive, supportive outcomes in a world where our very nature is designed to ward off threats and dangers. Trust is critical when building a high-functioning team. Dr. Azziz has built many high-functioning teams, and has centered on trust in three areas:

Trust of integrity. Can you rely on this person with confidence, and does this person have my best interests at heart? This type of trust must be demanded clearly and unequivocally from the start. It is the most critical element for leadership and team survival, yet the most fragile to endure.

Trust of ethics. Most of us assume that the ethics and morals of individuals who are at respective levels are already high. However, ethical trust is not just about whether the team members have passed background checks, it is about whether their moral compass is proper. Are they innately honest in all their dealings, whether as part of the organization or in their personal lives? Can we trust them to always do the right thing?

Trust of competence. Does the person have the skills necessary to accomplish the task? Are they insightful about their own limitations and knowledgeable about when to call for help?

GALLOP

The Gallop organization is famous for conducting surveys, and making meaning out of the results. For years they have been doing a survey for all kinds of organizations called the Twelve Elements of Great Managing. It may be advisable that you engage the Gallop organization to do the analytics of this survey, to help determine the level of employee trust in integrity, ethics and compassion. The scales are built around the following questions:

- I know what is expected of me at work.
- I have the materials and equipment I need to do my work right.
- At work, I have the opportunity to do what I do best every day.
- In the last seven days, I have received recognition or praise for doing good work.
- My supervisor, or someone at work, seems to care about me as a person.
- There is someone at work who encourages my development.
- At work, my opinions seem to count.
- The mission or purpose of my company makes me feel my job is important.
- My associates or fellow employees are committed to doing quality work.
- I have a best friend at work.
- In the last six months, someone at work has talked to me about my progress.
- This last year, I have had opportunities at work to learn and grow.

Can you respond with a positive answer to all those questions? If not, there may be trust missing from your team.

THE SPEED OF TRUST

We cannot do justice to the subject of trust without including the wonderful book The Speed of Trust by Stephen Covey. The book goes into great detail in many areas of trust, but centers on the following thirteen behaviors of a high trust leader. I read the book and heard Stephen speak, and he always asks the question, "Do you trust your boss?" The quickest way to lose trust is to violate a behavior of character, while the quickest way to increase trust is to demonstrate a behavior of competence.

Character Behaviors:

Talk straight. Simply, be honest and tell the truth. Let people know where you stand. Don't manipulate people or distort facts. Don't spin the truth, and don't leave false impressions.

Demonstrate respect. Respect the dignity of every person and every role. Behave in ways that demonstrate caring and concern. A good leader takes nothing for granted and recognizes the contributions made by everyone on the team. Think about specific things you can do to show others you care about them.

Create transparency. Transparency is about being open, real, genuine, and telling the truth in a way that people can verify. Disclose relationships, interests, and conflicts ahead of time so that everything is always out in the open.

Right wrongs. Don't let personal pride get in the way of doing the right thing. Make things right when you're wrong. Apologize quickly. Make restitution where possible. Practice service recoveries. Demonstrate personal humility. Don't cover things up.

Show Loyalty. Give credit to others and speak about people as though they were present. Represent others who aren't there to speak for themselves. Go out of your way to give credit to others. Don't badmouth others behind their backs, and don't disclose others' private information.

Competence Behaviors:

Deliver results. Get the right things done. Don't overpromise and under deliver. Don't make excuses for not delivering. Meet your commitments and accomplish what you are expected to do.

Get better. Continuously improve; increase your capabilities. Seek feedback and learn from mistakes. Don't assume your knowledge and skills will be sufficient for the future's challenges.

Confront reality. Address the tough issues. Share the bad news as well as the good. Lead courageously in controversial conversations. Don't ignore the real issues.

Clarify expectations. Create shared vision and agreement about what is to be done up front. Disclose and reveal expectations; discuss them. Renegotiate them if needed and possible. Don't assume expectations are clear or shared. Clarify expectations both at work and at home.

Practice accountability. Hold yourself and others accountable. Take responsibility for results. Don't blame others when things go wrong. Be clear on how you will communicate how you and others are doing.

Character and Competence Behaviors:

Listen first. Listen before you speak – understand and diagnose. Don't assume you know what matters most to others. Don't presume you have all the answers, or all the questions.

Keep commitments. Do what you say you are going to do. Make commitments carefully and keep them at all costs. Keeping commitments is your symbol of honor. Don't break confidences.

Extend trust. Demonstrate a propensity to trust. Extend trust to those who have earned it. Learn how to appropriately extend trust to others based on the situation, risk, character and competence of the people involved. Don't withhold trust because there is risk involved.

STEELCASE

I worked for Steelcase for several years, a great company where I had a wonderful experience. The hiring process was an example of mutual trust which reflected in the Human Resources team I worked with. It was the most thorough hiring process I have ever encountered – several interview trips, meeting with many people, department lunches, pre-hire assessments, and even an appointment with an industrial psychologist.

However, one vital element was missing. No one told me what the job was! I asked everyone I met, and they all told me to ask someone else. They would mention different things the job would likely be responsible for, but no title, and no job description.

After two fly-in, multi-day visits, I received a call from the search firm telling me that they want to fly me and my wife in together, and that is so they can make me the job offer. They always made their job offers in person. We made the arrangements, and I made the blunt statement that I was getting annoyed at not knowing the title of the job or seeing a job description – two very basic elements in the hiring process. Furthermore, I would not accept any job offer without seeing and discussing these very things. However, I was impressed with the company, the sophisticated level of Human Resources, the manager I would be working for, and the team members I would be working with. When we arrived we went into a conference room with the recruiting manager and my manager. I was told congratulations, we want to make you the offer to join our company. I responded that I want to accept, but would not do so until I am told what the job is, and see a job description. They both laughed and said no one could agree on that, it was a new position, and they understood that I was frustrated on the topic. They had defined many of their needs that they want someone to handle, and felt I was the right person to do it. So I was told if I accept the offer to join them, my first assignment would be to give myself a title and write my job description.

That is an example of a successful, professional relationship that started with mutual trust. They trusted me, that I would meet their needs for their undefined job. And I trusted them, that I could come and analyze their needs, and write my own job description.

NEVER SHAKE HANDS IN THE MENS ROOM

There was a scene in the old television show Boston Legal, when Candice Bergen's character was introduced into the series. They were all gathering at a fancy restaurant and she was anxious to meet James Spader. When someone said he was in the restroom, she walked right into the crowded men's room. Spader was just turning around from a urinal, and was startled by the encounter. She said she couldn't wait to meet him. Confused, he extended his hand to shake hands – to which she looked at his hand and asked "aren't you going to wash that first?"

Now there are several problems with this scene. First lesson of course is to always wash your hands after using the bathroom. Second – it was the men's room, and she should not have entered in the first place. Third, in a restroom, most people feel somewhat awkward and find it uncomfortable holding a meet and greet. And fourth, notwithstanding the often repeated scenes from old comedies where secret meetings were held in the men's room, it is the wrong place to conduct business.

We're still on the subject of trust here, and the men's room is merely symbolic. We trust that people use proper hygiene, because we are a culture of hand shakers. We trust that people will behave appropriately and not enter places that are off limits. We trust that people will not sneak away to share secrets. We trust that team members respect diversity, and thus would not conduct business in a place where members of the opposite sex are not allowed. And even when encounters do happen in the men's or women's rooms, wait to do the touching and further business conversation until you get outside. We need to trust, and we realize we are always vulnerable when we do.

CONFORMITY STUDIES

Through the 1950's and 60's Dr. Solomon Asch, founder of the Institute for Cognitive Studies, conducted a number of research studies on conformity. They are very entertaining You Tube hits. In the studies people would defy their own rational knowledge of what they knew was a correct answer, and go along with the incorrect opinions of others. This was done strictly out of peer pressure, or fear of being different. So they would submit their obvious incorrect answer in order to conform to the group.

Many decades earlier, in the 1890's, Ivan Pavlov, a Russian physiologist, conducted his research on classical conditioning. He won the Nobel Prize in 1904 for his famous "Pavlov's Dogs" studies where the dogs would salivate when hearing sound they associated with being fed.

Both of these experiments showed the world that people can be manipulated, tricked, and controlled. The people and dogs in the experiments trusted others and gave up their own logical, rational and correct thought process.

If you are a leader of people and use your position power or psychological influence to manipulate and control others into agreeing with you, or following you, rather than wanting them to express their honest opinions – please get out of management. The studies prove that you can manipulate people if you want to. But why would you want to? That's not leadership, that's narcissism.

And if you are a victim of such leadership, or team conspiracy, then you should get out. That is not the kind of environment you want to work for. There are many great companies and great leaders where your honest opinion will be desired, and where you have the freedom to disagree. Indeed, where disagreement will be valued. You want to associate with people who are deserving of your trust.

Chapter 19

The Places You'll Go

"I don't know what the future holds, but I know who holds the future." - Rev. Ralph Abernathy

We have identified the four ingredients necessary for achieving personal success – potential, attitude, energy and values. We also identified the ingredients necessary for driving team success – preparation, focus, passion and trust. Will they just happen naturally? Probably not. Are they almost impossible to achieve? Absolutely not. They can indeed be accomplished, but the ingredients for personal success must be made a dedication, and maintained as your modus operandi. The team ingredients must be communicated, implemented, collaborated and reinforced.

Once you have these elements in place, even though they will undergo breakdowns and restarts, it's time to have fun with it. Enjoy life and enjoy your accomplishments. These are the guidelines to ongoing satisfaction and successful outcomes. There is much to celebrate in the journey.

DR. SEUSS

Dr. Seuss was the penname for Theodor Seuss Geisel. He was a writer and illustrator. He worked for magazines, book publishers and advertising agencies. In 1954, Life magazine published a report on illiteracy among school children, which concluded that children were not learning to read because their books were boring. The director of education at the publishing firm where Ted Geisel was working challenged him to write a book using only 236 different first-grade words, and "bring back a book that children can't put down." With that assignment, Ted Geisel completed The Cat in The Hat.

By the time of his death in 1991, Geisel had written several of the most popular children's books of all time, selling over 600 million copies and being translated into more than 20 languages.

Oh, The Places You'll Go!
- Dr. Seuss

You have brains in your head.
You have feet in your shoes.
You can steer yourself
Any direction you choose.

You're on your own,
And you know what you know,
And you are the guy
Who'll decide where to go.

You'll be on your way up!
You'll be seeing great sights!
You'll join the high fliers
Who soar to high heights.

Wherever you fly, you'll be best of the best.
Wherever you go, you will top all the rest.

Oh, the places you'll go! There is fun to be done!
There are points to be scored. There are games to be won.
And the magical things you can do with that ball
Will make you the winningest winner of all.

So be sure when you step,
Step with care and great tact
And remember that life's
A great balancing act.

And will you succeed?
Yes! You will, indeed!
Ninety eight and three-fourths percent guaranteed.

As they say, the world is your oyster! You are free to do what you want to do, and how you want to do it. Do you have a bucket list? The bucket list concept is such a common expression and topic of conversations, yet I had never heard of the expression until the movie was made with that title. So it is basically "things I want to do before I die (kick the bucket)." However, I agree that everybody should have one, it is actually a different name for personal, fun-filled dreams and desires. Again, it is the purpose we have referred to. Draft your bucket list and keep it updated, it is your quest and your challenge. Bucket list items are things to plan for, budget for, and get excited about.

Some people have a long bucket list. I envy them. I seem to only have one item at a time. I guess I'm content, satisfied. But I do have passions – things I like to do and want to do. I do have goals. Interesting question, how does a bucket list differ from goals? Maybe goals become more fun and earn more focus when they make the bucket list. They reach a new level of criteria, and become more transparent. Goals can be private, a bucket list is usually shared. And bucket list items are for you personally, your own fun and fulfillment – not things like putting your kids through college. That's a goal.

I had one item on my bucket list. I wanted to play in a band on a stage and entertain people. I did that with our group The Happy Javelinas. Thus, my bucket list was completed, so I needed a next item.

Which became to write this book. I need to put more things on my bucket list – I'll work on that.

"When you can do the common things in life in an uncommon way, you will command the attention of the world."- George Washington Carver

Apply the ingredients for success to your personal job, to your team and company efforts, and indeed to your bucket list. Attack all with a sense of adventure and enthusiasm. That way your personal purpose and mission becomes fun, beneficial and attainable.

And as implied in the quote by George Washington Carver, do not be afraid to do things in an uncommon way. Make the challenge yours – you own it, you can make changes to do it in your own style. Inspire creativity in yourself and others.

We do our best to give guidance and inspiration to our children. We want them to excel and do wonderful things. However, I have heard many parents, maybe subconsciously, encouraging their kids to play it safe. Study a curriculum that you know will get a job. Take a job with an established firm. Don't propose something that may make you look unappreciative. Just do what you're told. Don't rock the boat.

The advice we should be giving is that as long as you stay true to your principles and values, and learn effective communicative skills, you can propose what you feel is right. Follow the course, and the leader, that inspires you. Be yourself, and enjoy life in your own way.

MAKE PEACE, NOT WAR

I have always managed people. I enjoy it, but not everyone does – I have often heard people say that they would never want to manage someone else. That's perfectly fine.

Before I was in Human Resources, I worked nine years in operations management. Maybe that is a reason I was effective in Human Resources, because I understood and appreciated the issues that operational people have to deal with. I graduated from Penn State in the college of Human Development. My first job out of college was at a state mental institution, where I was a dietitian and assistant to the director of the dietary department. We managed sixty people. Was I ready for that? Probably not, but I knew I had a lot to learn real fast. I did a lot of observation, and fortunately I had several good mentors, and the director to whom I reported took a sincere interest in my development.

One belief that came natural was the thought that everyone wants to do a good job, and be appreciated for it. I am convinced that people do not wake up in the morning with the intention of going to work and putting in a bad day of performance, upsetting their boss, making customers complain, and doing harm to the company.

Maybe it stems from my affinity for conflict avoidance. I do not like to get into conflict with others, and I do not like to see others in conflict. I try to prevent it, and when I see it happening I try to resolve it. I have at times been criticized for spending too much time and effort to settle a conflict, rather than being decisive and moving on, letting people either get over it or leave. Sometimes those criticisms were justified, but I would rather err on the side of compassion and hopefully having a positive outcome with all parties in better understanding and respect.

A sporting event can be an intense rivalry – but it is a game, not a war. A job is a livelihood, not a war. A work environment should feel secure, not threatening. Your home should be your sanctuary, not a battlefield. We all have the responsibility to create and ensure these positive atmospheres.

Some people seem to always be negative, they give the impression that they enjoy initiating conflict. You may have to deal with someone like this on a repeated basis. It takes a lot of diplomacy and tolerance to keep the upper hand. At some point they will have to be directly challenged. Such behavior destroys the harmony we have all worked so hard to develop, and we simply cannot allow the negative person to become divisive to the team.

"The future ain't what it used to be."- Yogi Berra

As you go through life and career, always keep your commitments – including those to yourself. I believe in giving 100% to your career, but as the old expression goes, "nobody was ever on their death bed wishing they would have spent more time at the office."

Work/life balance is a concept smart businesses provide for their employees. It is also a concept that smart people know is necessary for a fulfilling and complete lifestyle. It amazes me how there are still many people who do not even use their vacation time. You have to push them out for them to take time off. Then when you do, they spent the week finishing their basement or painting their garage. That's not a problem if that is their way of relaxing and enjoying their free time. But for some people, they encounter stress if they are not at work managing and controlling every activity – they have not developed the ability to trust others. That's not what life is all about.

Balance your life and stay open for opportunities. When I was given the opportunity to move into Human Resources, I found my perfect niche. Do your job well, keep a positive attitude, and opportunities will come.

"Funny now how it all went by so fast.
One day she's looking over her shoulder at the past,
When everybody had to go, had to be, had to get somewhere.
Somehow she forgot about what got her there."
- sung by Mary Chapin Carpenter

EPILOG

"I looked at life from both sides now,
from win and lose, and still somehow,
its life's illusions I recall,
I really don't know life at all."
- sung by Joni Mitchell

I have observed a lot through 40 years of Human Resources management, and 70 years of life. I have long felt my purpose in my chosen profession is to help make other people better. Therefore, my purpose in writing this book is to share my philosophies and beliefs to help you, the reader, achieve the success you are pursuing. I hope in some small way you have gleaned wisdom that you can apply in your personal or professional life.

Throughout the book I have shared some personal and historical stories, quotes, poetry, references to media productions and such. As you were reading, you probably related to some of your own experiences. Through these illustrations, we can see how it is common for people to depict stereotypical images of business (evil), government (incompetent), and management (foolish). Now realize that we are the business, we are the government, and we are the management. Our values and judgement have been influenced through our own stories and experiences; however, we have the power to reevaluate and change. We are responsible and accountable for knowing what is right and doing what is right. No more blaming our childhood, or our boss.

I want you all to experience the happiness and enrichment that comes with achieving personal success. The four ingredients that I have explained should serve as a guide for helping you get there.

Most of us serve on work teams at some point. Even if your occupation is that of an individual contributor or you are self-employed, you are still likely a participant on various types of teams. For these engagements I hope the team guidelines will serve to enhance your efforts for team success.

Now for a touch of reality. In your career and life, occasionally people will betray you. Most times it is unintentional, but still hurts. My advice is to take your personal high road – do not stoop to theirs. Follow your heart, stick to your values, adhere to your standard of right and wrong, follow your level of tolerance, and apply your sense of forgiveness. You will find success, in spite of the mess.

Celebrate

As the smoke clears, the dust settles, and the sun again shines, we see our Leader on a white horse. Thousands are cheering. There will be peace, prosperity and good times going forward. It doesn't matter if you are the one on the horse, or part of the cheering team. Together, we made it happen.